POETRY HISTORY MUSIC ART

POETRY HISTORY MUSIC ART

ESSAYS 1996-2017

LAURANCE WIEDER

Foreword by Herbert F. Tucker

ACKNOWLEDGMENTS

The lion's share of these essays were published by two magazine editors, J. Bottum of *First Things* and *The Weekly Standard*, and John Wilson of *Books & Culture*.

Both gave me the room to choose my own topics, and to write at length.

To both of them, thanks.

Copyright © 2019
Laurance Wieder
Foreword copyright © 2019
Herbert F. Tucker
All rights reserved

HIGH
LAND
BOOKS

ISBN: 978-1-7330907-1-1

COVER ART: William Wegman, from *Everyday Problems*
by permission of the artist
COVER DESIGN: Matthew Morse/ heymatthew.com

CONTENTS

FOREWORD 7
TOUCHING THE PRESENT 15
KNOWLEDGE AND MUSIC: Old Homer 21
DOWN TO THE SEA IN SHIPS: *The Children of Noah* 29
MONOTHEISM IN WORD AND MUSIC: *Moses und Aron* 37
THE GREAT GOOD PLACE: *Wozzeck* 43
UNQUIET SOULS: *The Peony Pavilion* 51
SPRINGTIME FOR WAGNER: *The Ring of the Nibelung* 57
CHEWING GUM: *American Poetry: The Twentieth Century* 67
EYE ALTERING: *William Blake* 77
INTO EGYPT: Along the Nile 87
PERFECTION. DESIRE. REGRET. *The Tale of Genji* 93
GUM ARABIC: Exiles 101
TURKISH MODERN: *Snow* 111
THE ORIGINAL TRUE HISTORY: *Don Quixote* 119
THE SERVICE: Poems for Yom Kippur 127
CONCEALED, REVEALED: *The Zohar* 133
CHINESENESS: *The Late Tang* 141
PLAINCLOTHES POLICEMEN OF LANGUAGE:
                               The Savage Detectives 147
WHEN MILTON SAYS 'SING' 155
AVATARS OF TRUE FEELING: *The Ramayana of Valmiki* 161
AN OLD MAN: *Taoteching* 173
TURKISH CLASSIC: Çelebi's *Book of Travels* 179
FAR FROM ME: Messiahs 187
CREDITS 199

FOREWORD

Wiederholung. Recitation.

Published over two decades, the essays in *Poetry History Music Art* have been reassembled by an author whose surname in German means "again".

Laurance Wieder's preferred occasion is the review. Ever curious about versions and renderings, he steadily discovers in the ostensibly secondary an inexhaustible originality. The poet recapitulating a known tradition and so changing it; the historian narrating fact or fiction in a chronicle or novel whose order freshly rearranges what has come to pass; the interpreter of an operatic score that itself interprets an antecedent tale or myth; the compiler and redactor and translator who indispensably co-create the inheritance they transmit; the cherisher of scriptural wisdom whose attentive care for the sacred text makes it new—these are Wieder's subjects, whose company he joins, as a delegate from our moment, in a fellowship of commentary that is world wide and millennia deep.

Commentary, not exegesis. Discussion, not explanation.

There's so much notice here of editions and translations, production history and provenance, because bibliography is textual biography, the life of the text *sine qua non*. When a work lives, in any medium, its inside and outside stories adjoin in a Möbius strip. Each supervening issue or comment, Wieder's included, forms in its time the latest episode in the long-range, slow-motion reception-history (Taoist, Homeric, Rabbinic...) of the work that prompts it.

The contextual material supplied here, the learning, is lightly carried, not stowed in footnotes but as part of the tour. It serves what these essays most aim to foster: direct encounter with a work which, no matter how elaborately mediated by first and subsequent responders, still packs a wallop.

To great art's capacity to stun and transport—or, in a minor corollary, mediocre art's disappointing failure at same—Wieder's prose seeks fit words of response, and few. The lapidary style of this book conveys neither diffidence nor routine modesty. Instead it vests strong faith in the reader's uptake, and with it hope that a hint well placed will arouse more responsive collaboration than would a fuller exegesis.

Faith, hope, and, greater than these, love.

When Wieder closes his review of *The Peony Pavilion* by weighing love against its look-alike, lore, scaling life against death, he puts in a nutshell the work that lore does throughout this book, which is to tend with vigilance "the source of poetry, and music, and intuition."

Because poetry "marks the place where understanding ends" (another parting shot, from "Gum Arabic"), lore or tuition stands to the intuitive openness of art as Dante's Virgil to his Beatrice, a guide through one sort of maze into a better sort—amazement—where understanding yields in love to imagination. Poetry "defies explanation" (thus "An Old Man" begins); when push comes to shove, this poet's prose does too.

For all Wieder's learned respect for history, *Poetry History*

Music Art is doubly emancipated from the historical order of straight chronology. The chapters follow neither the series of their composition between 1996 and 2017, nor the ancient-to-modern sequence of the works they discuss. Yesterday in Charlottesville precedes Homer and the Bible, Milton precedes the *Ramayana* and *Taoteching*. Such deliberate *Wiederholung* recites its message with the same difference that subsists between earlier and later moments in William Blake's eternity, practicing history in the prophetic key of (with a nice fillip to Ezra Pound) the "news that stays news, or will be."

Here, as in Roberto Bolaño's *The Savage Detectives*, poetry is "the only human thing that lasts": a definition that redounds on itself to confer poetic status on whatever persists in love's long and learned custody. *The Zohar*, *The Tale of Genji*, the deadeye reality transcripts of Evliya Çelebi's *Travels* command regard over the centuries because they disclose so much truth, which the Greeks called ἀλήθεια, because the *a-létheia* is the unforgotten.

The Lethe-proof moment lifted from secular oblivion is the renewable interval of creative encounter that these pages variously rehearse. Wieder's range and lightness of touch conjure a worldwide library of literature and gallery of art rendered, in accord with the kabbalistic messianism his final essay sketches, by "glyphs or emblems as well as in narrative." He welcomes anachronism (well-timed: yes, in Christopher Logue's post-Iliadic recruitment of the modern; no, in the Met's "overly topical" *Moses und Aron*) and relishes dissonance (well-tempered: Schoenberg's opera, also Berg's). Such rips in the tissue of the normal stir up truths normality conceals and disrupt time's drowsy flow with punctual alarms.

Art intervenes in the dream of the real so as to enable the restoration of "spiritual poise" (*The Peony Pavilion*) by "compelling the opposites to be visible" (Blake's method, and no less that of Homer and Wagner). Commentary that's worth keeping intervenes in art for the same purpose, showing yet again, like Daniel Matt's newly englished *Zohar*–and like *Poetry History Music Art*–that "both midrash and poetry are ancient novelties."

Where is the text, and when?

Once upon a time it was then and there; but always in order that it might come back to us here and now.

Eternity scandalizes clock time, and exile affronts fixed space. History and culture need to be unsettled if they are to survive our lethal certitudes, and rescue us as well.

–Herbert F. Tucker
John C. Coleman Professor of English
University of Virginia

POETRY HISTORY MUSIC ART

GREAT.

To buy a book, and then not read it;
To read it and not learn from it;
To learn, and never speak of it:
Tell me, what of the time spent?
Money is the least of it.

—L.W.

MUSIC ART

TOUCHING THE PRESENT

As a *darshan* (that is, interpreter) and occasional *maftir* or last reader at our lay-led, traditional egalitarian Sabbath services here in Charlottesville, Virginia, I am often struck by the immediacy of the Torah and *Haftarah* texts.

Sometimes Moses and the Prophets ascend from the mundane to the eternal; other times, their words reach down and touch the present.

Like Sabbath celebrants around the world, on August 12th, 2017, the morning minyan at Congregation Beth Israel in Charlottesville, read aloud in Hebrew from Deuteronomy 7:12-11:25, the Torah portion *Ekev* or "Because."

Unlike our fellow countrymen, we chanted

"How beautiful are your tents, O Jacob"

at an uncomfortable intersection of American politics and the history of our people.

Stonewall Jackson's statue stands one block east of our synagogue on Jefferson Street—at Fourth Street NE, near the courthouse. Not long ago, the courthouse park benches afforded an uncrowded spot to take a bag lunch (sunny in winter, shade in summer).

Robert E. Lee astride Traveller occupies the top of a grassy knoll two blocks west of the synagogue, across Second Street from the Historical Society and the Public Library, built on the original site of Beth Israel. This park between Jefferson and Market Streets, with its easy access to the Downtown Mall, has served as a campground for the homeless, and a place to play chess or music. Its prime location also has featured such events as a chocolate expo, and the Annual Festival of Cultures.

That Saturday, services began an hour early, so we might worship and depart the synagogue before scheduled demonstrations began at noon in the two parks with statues of men on horseback.

The congregation climbed the stairs of the main sanctuary on Jefferson Street, past a security line to enter through the only unlocked door.

During prayers, we heard the thump of helicopter rotors, crowds shouting and, from the windows outside the sanctuary, I watched groups of armed, uniformed neo-Nazis file down the Third Street sidewalk.

In *Ekev*, Moses asks Israel: What does the LORD your God require of you?

In his *Kuzari: An Argument for the Faith of Israel*, the Andalusian exile Hebrew poet Judah Halevi answered, that rational law, which demands justice, good actions, and recognizes God's bounty, rules every community. The Torah is corollary to rational law. Without Israel's knowing how, the Presence descended and God's fire consumed their offerings. Israel heard God speak, heard the story of their becoming a people—all matters which reason would refuse, unless affirmed by observance.

"Is it enough," Halevi asked, "for Jews to practice doing justice and love mercy? Can they neglect circumcision, Sabbath, and other laws, and still feel happy?"

Following the Torah portion and before the scroll was returned to the ark, we heard Isaiah 49:14-51:3, a *Haftarah* of consolation. This day, although the blessings were chanted in Hebrew, the selection was read in English.

After services, we gathered in the hall adjacent the main sanctuary to sing the customary verses instructing Israel to keep the Sabbath; prayers were spoken over wine and bread, and the Rabbi announced that "the Torahs have been removed to a safe place."

The congregation left the house of learning in small groups.

With my wife and two friends, we walked along Fourth Street back to the car.

Our view of Stonewall Jackson was obscured by the crowd. Some wore message t-shirts, some wore camouflage, one was dressed as Captain America. Many carried weapons.

As we waited at the red light, a pick-up truck with rolled-up tinted windows honked, several times.

Hard to tell who belonged to whom.

Driving home on Ninth Street, I saw six men and one woman get out of a white van. Dressed in black body armor and Darth Vader helmets, they unloaded assault rifles, batons and shields from the back of their van. All wore sidearms.

While I in the back seat recalled anti-war marches from the nineteen-sixties, from behind the wheel Sam the frequent *Shacharit* talked about his days as a police cadet in Colorado thirty years ago.

I was angry and afraid.

None of us wanted to pick up a gun.

How then to speak about the unspeakable, in credible language, when reason refuses and politics fails? A pointed question in the little city of Thomas Jefferson, the slaveholder author of the Declaration of Independence, whose Monticello was purchased by Commodore Uriah Levy, and restored by his nephew, New York Jewish congressman Jefferson Monroe Levy.

At the end of his consolation in the *Haftarah*, Isaiah offers first this:

> Look, all you who kindle fire,
> > who wield torches,
>
> depart in the flames of your fire,
> > by the flares you ignited.
>
> By my hand, this for you:
> > where you lie down is terror.

And, because a *Haftarah* must conclude with a blessing, the prophet closes with this instruction:

> Hear me, you who pursue justice,
> > who seek the LORD:
>
> Look to the rock you were hewn from,
> > the pit where you were quarried.
>
> Look to Abraham your father,
> > and to Sarah who bore you.
>
> Only one when I called him,
> > I blessed him, and made him many.

MUSIC ART

> For the Lord comforts Zion,
> > comforts all her desolations;
> he will make her wilderness like Eden,
> > her desert like the LORD's garden.
> Joy and pleasure are found in her,
> > thanksgiving and the voice of song.

KNOWLEDGE AND MUSIC: Old Homer

War Music, Christopher Logue's "account" of Homer's *Iliad*, proves (again) that poetry is the fit medium for truth. And great entertainment.

Logue's late-twentieth-century fragment stands atop all our inherited versions of Homer, the linguistic equivalent of Schliemann's Troy. His new-made *Iliad* in English verse has the freedom and vigor of an extraordinarily gifted and beautiful child of old, moneyed family. Guiltlessly, the poet deploys his historical and vernacular inheritance to create an *Iliad* that's not held hostage by yearning for the Greek.

The Trojan War was a struggle between East and West, between tribes (the Balkan Greeks) and empire (the Trojan Medes), between raw impulse and high civilization. Events in *The Husbands*, Logue's third installment of Homer's original (after *War Music* and *Kings*), organize around the duel between Menelaos and Paris, Helen's "husbands" and the injured parties in the war.

Here's Paris:

> Napoleon's Murat had 50 hats
> And 50 plumes each 50 inches high
> And 50 uniforms and many more
> Than 50 pots of facial mayonnaise
> Appropriate to a man with tender skin;
> He also had 10,000 cavalry,
> Split-second timing, and contempt for death.

> So Providence—had he been born
> Later and lowlier—might well have cast Prince Paris.
> The centuries have not lied:
> Observe the clotted blossoms of his hair,
> Frost white, frost bright—and beautifully cut,
> Queen Aphrodite's favourite Ilian....

Here's Menelaos charging with his spear:

> In a fast slouch, the Trojan lord,
> With a belligerent snarl, the Greek,
> Come on to it.
> Both men stand tall. Both men look large
> And though the Ilians were proud of him,
> Paris, his mirror bronze, his hair,
> Beautiful as he was, they detested him.
> But heroes are not frightened by appearances.
> Under his breath Lord Menelaos says:
> "I hate that man. I am going to kill that man.
> I want to mark his face. I want to shout into his face:
> You are dead. You are no longer in this world."

The heroes' stature, by the way, is a running joke. Logue puts Paris' height the same as Hector's—8'9". Priam, we're told in this book, stands 8'6". But in *Kings* (Books 1 and 2), the King of Troy is 6'6" tall. Those epic vitamins.

What of the motive, Helen? Aphrodite tells her as she bathes:
> "You wear a crown of hearts. Your duty is
> To stir and charm the wonder of the world.
> To raise the cry: Beauty is so unfair!"

> Leaves. Tiles. The sky. "And so it is.
> Free. And unfair. And strong. A godlike thing."
> The water's net across the water's floor.

In Logue's account, the erotic suffices as a cause for war. Also, the conflicting intentions of human and gods are represented as something more compelling than a classroom rubric. Even the *deus-ex-machina* sleight-of-hand that spirits Paris from the field before Menelaos can finish him off is handled like the dazzling stage effect it is, rather than a verbal formula.

Except for George Chapman's Homer (a great Elizabethan poem) and Alexander Pope's *Iliad* (a work of high polish and manners), and this one, other versions of Homer in English verse and prose walk shackled by ideas about the Greek.

Prose retelling doesn't work, period. *The Iliad* is not a novel, is more than its plot, and prose requires the engine of a plot to move along. Poetry's engine turns in the verse.

Verse *Iliads* in English have set out to relate the story, or to render word-for-word, or to recreate some aspect of the old Greek such as its word order, rhythm or measure. This requires a willing suspension of disbelief in our native language; knowledge and judgement and nuance and all those voices heard that make the tongue a vehicle for the living spirit have to make way for a labored impossibility. The reader must believe that the 3,000-year-old past is present, that Homer writes in English, and that his dialect (never spoken) knows of nothing that has happened in the intervening millennia. What this leads to can be found in almost any Hollywood film on a classical theme: think of all those Hercules movies; think of *Clash of the Titans*.

Poetry vibrates between two extremes. At one pole, the poem is a poem because of what it knows. At the other extreme, the poem is poetry because of how it says what it says. The knowledge and music, inseparable in the original, become analytic, visible choices in the translation. For examples of these extremes, look at any renderings from the Chinese into English of Tu Fu on the one hand and Li Po on the other. Translations of Dante and Petrarch afford another example. By Matthew Arnold's account, Homer is at once saying and knowing, swift and direct. Ideas about the language of the original poem are a downright impediment to making an English version that's poetry. Poetry's material is the (written) word, as the material of movies is shadow, light and sound. The whole formal and conventional apparatus only exists to preserve and transmit a living voice. Ideas do not make poetry, just like stars and deals do not make movies and remarks, however earnest, are not literature.

Rather than pretend to know how Homer struck his contemporaries—which is another version of that old scholastic question, What song did the Sirens sing?—Christopher Logue takes Homer as a foundation, a given. Wherever it finally stops, Logue's work will look complete, because at least in the bold outline, everything is already known and he, a master of metonymy, can build whatever he wants on the plains of Troy and rest assured the work will stand strong as marble columns in a dreamscape.

In loose blank verse akin to that employed by Milton in *Paradise Regained*, Logue marshals all the imaginative resources available to an educated, sentient person at the end of the 20th century. His narrator doesn't pretend to be a bronze-age blind bard. He knows better than to test his popular audience with catalogues and battles crowded with the genealogies and particularized deaths of heroes whose only purpose is to fall. Logue's Homer has more sense than to weight the flight of his song down with repeated epithets that might have helped a singer of tales to keep the thread and to improvise, but which only clog and spoil writing. His visualizations have the sweep and scale of wide-screen movies; constraints of time and space are illusions of the gods, for us. Homer's Greek and Trojan heroes act and speak and are alive and believable without apology or special permit. Their motives, and the gods they pray to, are credible and moving.

Living and writing in the late twentieth century has its burdens as well as its privileges. The telescoped time of this simile as the armies square off fuses the melancholy of history with the sadness of nature:

> Think of the noise that fills the air
> When autumn takes the Dnepr by the arm
> And skein on skein of honking geese fly south
> To give the stateless rains a miss:
> So Hector's moon-horned, shouting dukes
> Burst from the tunnels, down the slope,
> And shout, shout, shout, smashed shouted shout
> Backwards and forth across the sky;
> While pace on pace the Greeks came down the counterslope
> With blank, unyielding imperturbability.

Or here, as the Greeks and Trojans under truce settle down to watch the duel between Menelaos and Paris:

> Now dark, now bright, now watch—
> As aircrews watch tsunamis send
> Ripples across the Iwo Jima Deep,
> Or, as a schoolgirl makes her velveteen
> Go dark, go bright—
>   The armies as they strip, and lay their bronze
>   And let their horses cool their hooves
>   Along the opposing slopes.

Old Homer is the vehicle not only for the story of Troy, but also for most of what is known about Greek mythology, pre-history, geography, religion, and the arts. Logue doesn't try to bring all this baggage aboard his bark; he brings to his poem some knowledge Homer didn't have. For him (that is Logue) to abjure the last 2500 years would be to lobotomize his enterprise. Why have a tool that will do a job, and not use it? One might compose music in the late 20th century for Renaissance period instruments, but it would always be, like theme park castles, a replica and qualified, rather than authentic. *Kings*, *The Husbands* and *War Music*, *All Day Permanent Red* and *Cold Calls*, (the discrete parts of Logue's homeric ruin) make a compelling epic. I can participate in the work emotionally and esthetically and intellectually without reservation. It sings *a capella*. Its theme is not concocted.

If David's *Psalms* give individuals language for emotions and obligations and joys and predicaments predicated upon the Fall of

Man and the Law, then Homer's poem is of the other eternity. There, gods are just like men who live forever, and can do what they please. Nobody knows what they have in mind. The godlike heroes do what they must, and die. Greeks and Trojans pray convincingly to gods who do or do not listen, and who themselves divide things into two: not good and evil, life and death, but them and us. Unlike the *Psalms*, the *Iliad* takes no sides. Terror and pity course through both Greeks and Trojans; for Homer as well as for Logue, what survives is knowledge and music.

DOWN TO THE SEA IN SHIPS: *The Children of Noah*

Sigmund Freud apostrophized religion as the oceanic feeling; the sea itself opposed the work of creation according to ancient myth. Aside from the stories of Noah, and Jonah, two chapters of Ezekiel, and passages in the Psalms and Job, sailors receive scant notice in the Old Testament. In *The Children of Noah: Jewish Seafaring in Ancient Times*, Raphael Patai contends that sea travel was no rarity for the Children of Israel. Rather, once they gained access to the coast, the Hebrews "learned to use the sea as a path to other lands in a manner no different from that of other circum-Mediterranean cultures."

An anthropologist, Raphael Patai (who died in 1996) was also a Talmudic scholar and an ordained rabbi. He wrote more than thirty books over his sixty-year career, anatomies with such titles as *Man and Temple in Ancient Jewish Myth and Ritual*, *On Culture Contact and Its Working in Modern Palestine*, *Women in the Modern World*, *The Republic of Lebanon*, *The Kingdom of Jordan*, *The Messiah Texts*, *Gates to the Old City* (a compendium of Jewish legends), and *The Jewish Alchemists*. His *The Hebrew Goddess*, a scholarly investigation of archaic polytheistic elements of Judaism and the persistence of the mother goddess in the Talmudic and cabbalistic guises, informed Robert Graves' *The White Goddess*. Graves and Patai subsequently collaborated on *Hebrew Myths: The Book of Genesis*.

Despite their number, range and thematic richness, Raphael Patai's books have never received anything like the notice accorded Gershom Scholem's studies of Jewish Kabbalah and messianism.

Scholem's works of scholarship tower inside the eternal city of Jewish scholarship, which regards much modern thought with the same dismissal that Jesus voiced when Satan tempted him with gentile learning in *Paradise Regained*. *Major Trends in Jewish Mysticism*, *Origins of the Kabbalah*, *Sabbatai Şevi: The Mystical Messiah*, and *The Mystical Shape of the Godhead* originate in and ultimately refer to texts and ideas rather than to social life. This hermeticism, and the exercise of his ferocious learning, stamp Scholem's books with power, and glamour, and difficulty, with scholar's pride.

Raphael Patai's books are more modest in demeanor. Rooted in the empirical, they put material ahead of ideas about the material. Asking how things are actually done is thoroughly Talmudic, but answering inquiries about biblical details with examples from outside Judaism, and outside Israel, is not so usual. For example, in his chapter in *Children of Noah* on boatbuilding, (which might have appeared in *Wooden Boat* magazine or *Scientific American*), Patai remarks that the practice of shading the cockpit of a vessel with a wattle canopy survives to this day in southeast Asia.

Like Scholem's, Patai's life work turns about a major theme: that the people apart have always lived in a larger context. Nothing comes of nothing. Israel's myths, laws, rituals, kinship systems, trade practices, were drawn from the same wells as the surrounding nations. It implies considerable fortitude, to escape the holocaust which separated out even those who thought themselves assimilated, and then hold to a scholarly course which basically says, from a host of perspectives, that no one is exempt.

Expanding the incomplete historical picture of ancient Jews as a landlocked people, *The Children of Noah* assembles data from a wide variety of Near Eastern, Jewish and Hellenic sources, from the earliest records down to the year 500 CE. The number of ancient texts is finite, so the pertinent information Patai gleaned from the harvest makes an elegant volume. An appendix, "Biblical Seafaring and The Book of Mormon," by John M. Lundquist, connects Patai's subject with the Mormon tradition that a group of Jews sailed west through the Straits of Gibraltar in 589 BCE, three years before Nebuchadnezzar destroyed Jerusalem and made Judah captive.

The great boat Utnapishtim built in the *Epic of Gilgamesh* according to the direction of the god Ea was a huge cube, measuring 120 cubits (180 feet) in each direction. Noah, the first shipbuilder, also received instruction from the divine architect:

> Make thee an ark of gopher wood; rooms shalt thou make in the ark, and shalt pitch it within and without with pitch. And this is the fashion which thou shalt make it of: The length of the ark shall be three hundred cubits, the breadth of it fifty cubits, and the height of it thirty cubits. A window shalt thou make to the ark, and in a cubit shalt thou finish it above; and the door of the ark shalt thou set in the side thereof; with lower, second, and third stories shalt thou make it. (Genesis 6:14-16)

Patai wonders, What did the ark look like? How was it made?

My facsimile copy of *The Geneva Bible* (1560) has a line engraving of Noah's Ark on page 3. Rain pours from the clouds, the seas rise above treetops covering a city and mountain in the background, while about the ark in the surrounding waves are the heads and raised arms of the drowning. The ark itself is a three-story rectangular solid, 300 cubits by 50 cubits by thirty cubits high, with a second-story entrance, more bargelike than the great Babylonian cube, and not so shipshape as the ark shown on page 12 of *Picture Stories from the Bible* (1942), the Old Testament in comic-strip form, where it looks like a double-ended dory with a deal cabin plonked on its deck.

The talmudist reasons that the ratio between height, length and width of Noah's ark correspond to the length, beam, freeboard and draft of ancient war galleys. He reproduces pictures of a Roman galley from a relief in the Vatican, a sailing ship on a Hebrew seal from the eighth to seventh century BCE, a sketch of a ship from a catacombs near Haifa, and a sketch of a ship from a city southwest of Jerusalem in the third century BCE, which suggest aspects of Noah's great ship. Acknowledging that the dimensions of the Biblical ark (450 feet long, 75 feet wide, 45 feet high) must have been exaggerated in order to be equal to its task of transporting all those animals, Patai notes that Utnapishtim's ark was reported by Berosus, a Babylonian historian, to be 100 yards long, and 400 yards wide. One version of Eusebius' *Chronicles* states the Akkadian ark was nearly two miles long.

Other questions Patai asks and answers in his first chapter include: What is gopher wood?—Lebanese cedar. Pitch?—Bitumen. What was the window (*tzohar*) in the ark (a question which baffled the Rabbis, who thought it might be a pearl hung in the ark that shone for all the creatures in it like a candle that shines in the house, and like the sun at noon.) What about waste disposal?

Accommodations? Navigation?

Noah's dove, who was sent three times to find dry land after the rain stopped (Genesis 8:8), does the work assigned to a dove, a swallow and a raven in the Gilgamesh story. Citing a study by James Hornell called "The Role of Birds in Early Navigation," Patai records that ancient Hindu merchants used "shore-sighting birds" to locate land on overseas voyages. So did the sailors of first century Ceylon, according to Pliny, because they were not able to steer by the stars.

As in any work that is at heart a catalogue, this book affords most pleasure in the details. For example, the sages describe a boat tapering downward toward its keel as 'a dancing ship.' Patai expounds: "Rabbi Yohanan's laconic statement that the bread [offered up in the Temple] was shaped 'like a dancing ship,' is explained by Rashi: such a ship 'has no brims, but is wide at the top and narrow toward the bottom until it has only the thickness of a finger. Its ends sharpen and rise upward and do not touch the water, and that is why she is called "dancing," because she dances along quickly.'"

Patai continues, "The question of how ship-shaped (V-shaped) loaves of bread could stand up without falling to the side is raised and answered in a passage in the Midrash: 'The loaves were in the shape of ships, and therefore they had to be propped up with oblique supports...but the middle of the lowest loaf touched the table, for the loaf was like a dancing ship which is narrow at the bottom, broadening upward.'"

The anthropologist-rabbi finds information on ships' crews in Isaiah, Proverbs and Acts. Maritime trade practices are adduced from verses in the Books of Moses and Judges. Life on the high seas is depicted in Talmudic commentary on First Kings. The slightest of allusions hint at naval warfare in biblical sources, but Josephus gives a close account of the catastrophic encounter between the Jewish fleet and Vespasian's navy.

A chapter on "Laws of Sea and River" details commercial arrangements as well as efforts to adapt Jewish ritual requirements to the sailor's life. The chapter collecting similes and parables itemizes sand and sea in Old Testament similes and in the Talmud, and similes for ships. There I found such sentences as, "Much Torah did I learn, and yet I did not subtract from [the learning of] my masters even as much as a dog licking from the sea;" and "The beauty of the waves was deemed of a higher order than that of golden decorations."

In the chapter of "Sea Legends and Sailors' Tales," Patai recalls the biblical legends of the sea resisting the creation, of Leviathan and other sea monsters. In the Talmud, the sea spares the righteous, gives and takes, threatens and punishes, converts idolators, all in a spirit easily recognized from folk tales.

The penultimate chapter outlining Red Sea and Mediterranean ports serves as an antiquarian's Baedeker, locating and describing the places alluded to in Biblical, Hellenic and Talmudic sources.

Patai's last chapter takes as its subject Lake Kinneret, also known as Lake Gennesareth, the Sea of Galilee, or the Sea of Tiberias. Israel's only major freshwater lake figures large in the Gospels. It was mentioned in Numbers, Deuteronomy, and is the site of three fortified cities named in Joshua: Hammath (called Emmaus by Josephus); Rakkath, identified with Tiberias or Sephoris; and

Kinneret (in Roman times rebuilt as Gennesareth.)

The chapter concludes with a photograph of a fishing boat from the beginning of the Christian era found in the mud of Lake Kinneret. The craft had been constructed of cedar planks joined by mortise and tenon, nailed to ribs made from naturally curved oak branches. As an emblem to accompany Raphael Patai's last word on any subject, it fits: practical rather than musical, empirical rather than imperious, durable rather than glamorous—yet for all that a vessel with spirit, freighter of mysteries.

MUSIC ART

MONOTHEISM IN WORD AND MUSIC: *Moses und Aron*

Arnold Schoenberg had a superstitious horror of the number thirteen. He was born on September 13, 1874, the day after Rosh Hashanah. A Viennese Jew reared as a Catholic, he converted to Lutheranism in his twenties, before returning to Judaism in 1933. Schoenberg's opera *Moses und Aron*, based on passages in the books of Exodus and Numbers, was composed using the twelve-tone method he invented. He spelled Aaron with one "A" so his opera's title wouldn't have thirteen letters—though the plot summary provided by New York's Metropolitan Opera for its new production locates Act One of *Moses und Aron* in the "thirteenth century, B.C."

Few lives in art were more dogged by contradiction and controversy than Arnold Schoenberg's. Recognized as a genius from an early age, he could have fashioned success in the manner of Richard Strauss. Or he could have assumed the legacy of Gustav Mahler, composing huge orchestral and choral works as he did with the epic folk-song cycle, *Gurrelieder* (1900). Schoenberg even composed naughty songs for the turn-of-the century Viennese cabaret. But with more and more insistence, "the dissonance" repressed inside the conventional language of music was clamoring for release from those harmonic rules that "required" music to end in the key in which it had begun. Harmony signals resolution, a neatness in the packaging, a pat solution that could no longer claim to be more than a fiction. And that became intolerable to Schoenberg, who regarded music as a vehicle for truth and himself as its reluctant emancipator.

From 1900 to 1913, Schoenberg's compositions (and those of his students Alban Berg and Anton Webern) grew stranger and stranger to Viennese ears. In 1912, Schoenberg finished *Pierrot Lunaire*, a song cycle that still sounds like the future. In February 1913, his *Gurrelieder* was staged in Vienna to great acclaim. The next month, a performance of his more recent works provoked a riot. To the end of his life, Schoenberg drew the fire of critics and a middlebrow public that went to concerts for reassurance and relaxation, to be lulled instead of invited to think. It might have been the dissonance initially. But something more set the wasps about Schoenberg. Igor Stravinsky, Claude Debussy, Bela Bartok, and Richard Strauss exploited the new continent of dissonance opened by Schoenberg and found themselves embraced by audiences.

In the 1920s, Schoenberg constructed a compositional system to replace traditional key signatures with a series of twelve tones that defined and generated a musical piece. The tone row (or series) is no less arbitrary than traditional harmony, but it gave the composer's musical instincts a shield against the chaos implied by the fall of the old musical gods and a way of answering the critics who assailed him for his method even as they reviled his compositions.

To say that Schoenberg was a Moses, emancipating dissonance and leading music toward a land he would not enter might be neat, but it doesn't answer why *Moses und Aron*, written explicitly as an invitation to think, is such powerful music theater, against commercial pieties and all the other odds.

Schoenberg wrote the libretto of his 1932 biblical opera in three acts, but he only set the first two acts to music. In the following years, as prospects for its performance evaporated, the composer suggested that Act Three might be omitted or merely read aloud. Or, should resources preclude a full production, Schoenberg wryly suggested that the "Dance Around the Golden Calf" in Act Two might be performed as a stand-alone piece. In any case, the prophet of serial composition and model for the protagonist of Thomas Mann's *Doktor Faustus* died on Friday, July 13, 1951, having never witnessed a staging of his masterpiece. Monday, February 8, 1999, after more than forty years of wandering, *Moses und Aron* entered the promised land: a premiere production at the Metropolitan Opera at Lincoln Center.

It opened to a full house. No one left before the first act, and most of the audience stayed for the second. This was itself a wonder, since the New York public customarily walks out of a concert hall at the first strange sound, the exodus to dissonance. The orchestra, directed by James Levine, played Schoenberg's score as music rather than as a lecture or demonstration. The huge chorus sustained the music and provided a context for the action. Moses, sung with clarity and conviction by British basso John Tomlinson in his Metropolitan debut, had a real beard. The spare, expressive stage set designed by Paul Brown used only blue and orange-red to relieve its black and white, and a few shapes—wedge, wave, and bowl—to suggest Mount Horeb, the desert, the sky, Egypt, and Sinai. Costumes were modern street dress: black and white suits and dresses, shoes, plus some hats, and furs, and watches and jewels. In the tradition of Bertolt Brecht's Berlin theater, each scene was identified by a caption printed on a piece of scenery.

Act Two takes place in Moses' absence. After an orchestral interlude, Schoenberg's libretto calls for the overthrow of the elders of Israel, the exaltation of the Golden Calf on the Altar, the sacrifice of herds of animals followed by a dance of the ritual slaughterers, a faith healing, suicides, renunciation, murder, orgies of drunkenness and dancing, the sacrifice of four naked virgins, then a general stripping to shouted slogans praising creative power, fertility, and desire.

The Met production took some liberties with the libretto. First, it updated the dancing. As choreographed by Ron Howell, the herds are gone; butchers and leaders of the tribes of Israel and their followers became fashion models and bulb-popping photographers, businessmen and politicians, gangsters and teenagers chewing gum. The people who followed their prophet into the wilderness in Act One, dressed like any prosperous crowd of upper-West-Side Manhattanites, became overly specific, overly topical. I found myself remembering the musical toughs in *West Side Story* instead of hanging on the action. As the flashbulbs popped and cash was spread around, I wondered when they'd get to the naked virgins already, and would the Metropolitan Opera pull its punches?

Schoenberg, in a performance footnote, demanded nakedness "insofar as the law and the needs of the stage permit and demand." The Met's virgins did peel, down to their undies; as did all the other naked people called for in the stage directions. I'm not sure whose rules and needs were being heeded. No New York audience would have been shocked by total nudity, and maybe if naked had meant naked, the New Yorkers might have actually felt rebuked by Moses' descent from the mountain. Spared that self-scrutiny, the dancing and cavorting before the Golden Calf—the entertainment for its own sake—proved thin gruel.

Act Two has much in common with cabaret or music hall. Besides strippers and naked dancers, it features stand-up comedians, tellers of quiet jokes. The renouncers and sacrificers give away what they don't have, or don't need, or don't want, in sacrifice to an inanimate object that can't use it anyway. The virgins give their passion; old people sacrifice the remainder of their lives; the poor donate their sad rags to the gods of self. Schoenberg's figurative witticisms are like the jokes in Freud's *Wit and its Relation to the Unconscious*: examples of behavior, pointed demonstrations or mild provocations to something other than laughter. In a peculiar variation on a song-and-patter routine (in this instance, an invention of the Met's), the compromised Elders of Israel dropped their trousers and put shoes on their hands, so that they appeared to dance, upside down, the old soft shoe.

More than the Elders got stood on their heads. It would be reasonable to expect that song and dance, orgy and riot, bloodshed and spectacle would be more of a show than the anguished and self-consuming philosophical and theological dialogue of two brothers, but they aren't. Schoenberg's representation of theology in word and music beggars everything else in the opera. In *Moses und Aron*, thought carries the day; high art and religion make livelier theater than do the staples of entertainment. On this stage, virtue plays better than sin.

Dissonance, for Schoenberg, meant more than music theory. It referred as well to the moral uncertainty that accompanies the discovery that the world is not adequately described in terms of the self. It is Moses' recognition that the Land of Milk and Honey doesn't exist except as a promise, and Aron's problem that when Israel hears the promise, they want it fulfilled. Made to wait, they seek refuge in the gods they know, gods like themselves. It is the uncomfortable intuition that people may choose freedom, but they desire bondage. Dissonance is embedded in the materials of language and art, because neither language nor art penetrates to reality, the thing-in-itself. Dissonance in Schoenberg's hands invokes a belief in meaning beyond the self, at the same time acknowledging it's just the self that knows.

Opera isn't usually an arena for hard thinking. It is typically loved for grand passions realized in gorgeous fantasy, for impossibilities enacted in librettoland. It is multimedia fairy tale music videos for grown-ups. *Moses und Aron* offers a different kind of adult entertainment. It refutes the assertions that there's no such thing as art, that no thought is higher than another. One clear voice can carry over a chorus, and an evening of opera can stay in the head as something other than a melody and masquerade.

Schoenberg uses the imaginative freedom granted by the operatic suspension of disbelief if not to justify then at least to engage God's ways to man. His is the drama of monotheism, the song of the limited self in an infinite universe, of freedom and awe, bondage and security, the dance of the young who would be old and the old who would be young.

Moses und Aron is stronger than pleasure.

THE GREAT GOOD PLACE: *Wozzeck*

Alban Berg's *Wozzeck* is grand opera through the back door. The characters are unlovely, the costumes plain, the arias atonal, the plot bare, the speeches nearly unconnected, the orchestra rather than the characters makes sense of the action. This story of a plain soldier's love-murder-suicide told in the language of twelve-tone music was instantly hailed as a masterpiece at its first performance at the Berlin State Opera House in 1925. The two Metropolitan Opera productions I've seen—in the 1970s and again in 1999—confirm the opera's place in the canon.

How the story came to the stage is itself a story.

In 1821, Johann Christian Woyzeck, an itinerant wigmaker, barber, illuminator of copper engravings, and sometime soldier murdered his mistress in a jealous rage. He was immediately arrested, tried two months later and sentenced to death. On appeal, the defense mounted an insanity defense—a novelty for the time, especially when applied to a 31-year-old drifter. Witnesses came forward to attest to Woyzeck's derangment. A detailed medical examination into the murderer's state-of-mind was conducted. Found to be suffering from hallucinations and voices, but otherwise healthy, Woyzeck was beheaded in the Leipzig public square before a curious crowd. Professional debate about the medical examiner's judgement continued well into the 1830s. Some said the murderer was mentally disturbed. Others described his symptoms as "moral decrepitude."

Georg Büchner, a German medical student and writer who died of typhus in 1837 at the age of 23, followed this curious case in the professional journals. Among his literary remains was a manuscript draft and supplementary sketches for a play, *Woyzeck*, which incorporated Woyzeck's accounts of his visions and the medical testimony directly into speeches of the evolving drama. Though his collected works were published in one volume in 1850, the manuscript notes and fragments of Büchner's unfinished text moldered forgotten in a trunk for 38 years after the author's death. Karl Emil Franzos, a prolific Jewish novelist, deciphered, transcribed and published what Büchner called his "swinish" play in a Viennese newspaper in 1875.

Büchner's drama finally reached the stage in 1913, in Munich, as *Wozzeck*. (The name change was an artifact of the illegibility of the original manuscript.) Alban Berg attended the Viennese premiere in May, 1914 and, according to a man who sat in the row in front of him, the composer left the theater visibly moved. "Someone," Berg said, "must set this to music."

Alban Berg was one of Arnold Schoenberg's two great disciples in the emancipation of dissonance (which was musical candor) and devotion to serial composition as a means of articulating musical truth (the other disciple was Anton Webern.) The Viennese Berg, like his fellow citizens the dramatist Frank Wedekind (whose Lulu plays he would also set to music), Karl Kraus, playwright and editor of *Der Fackel*, and the father of psychoanalysis Sigmund Freud, regarded sex as the central fact of human nature, and celebrated the direct confrontation of the self.

Although he set about his task directly, Berg was famously slow at his work. Indeed, he stopped assigning opus numbers to his compositions because, he said, he felt ashamed at how few works he had composed over the years. In the case of *Wozzeck*, however, events forestalled him. Called up for military service between 1915 and 1917, Berg had an opportunity to taste the humiliation of an infantry private first-hand. In a letter, he asked, "Have you ever heard a lot of people all snoring at the same time? The polyphonic breathing, gasping and groaning makes the strangest chorus I have ever heard. It is like a music of the primeval sounds that rises from the abysses of these people's souls."

Following his military discharge, Private Berg returned to work. Alban Berg pretty much took the text for his libretto as he found it in the production he'd seen before the war. As he composed, the work organized itself into an opera in three acts of five scenes, each scene a discrete piece of music in classical form. Some material was dropped, some condensed.

The five scenes of Act 1 establish Wozzeck's living conditions and inner state, his hallucinations (as reported in the trial literature) and the views of his military superior, the regimental doctor, the yearnings of his mistress Marie, and the sexual power of the drum major. Act 2 reveals Marie's betrayal to Wozzeck, his humiliation at the hands of his Captain and the doctor, and the drum major's flaunting his conquest at the beer garden and in the barracks. Act 3 plays out the tragedy. Marie reads the story of Mary Magdalene. Wozzeck takes her out for a walk, and stabs her. He returns to the tavern with blood on his hands. He flees, and drowns himself in a pond near Marie's corpse. Following an orchestral epilogue, children tell Marie's child that his mother is dead.

To Webern, Berg confessed in a letter that "I cannot say whether or not I am pleased with what I have written, but I do feel warmth in writing it, and it runs from my hand more easily than I would have thought after such a long break... What touches me so closely is not only the fate of this poor man persecuted and exploited by the all the world, but also the unbelievably concentrated mood of the individual scenes..."

This concentration of mood, or effect, in Wozzeck is accomplished entirely through the music, which sets the original text not in the sense of a jewel set in metal to display its qualities, or a fencepost set in cement to keep it upright, but rather the music is the medium of life and imagination, of creatures set in a garden. It endows Büchner's fragment with logic and coherence and heart, and imparts (in the long orchestral meditation that precedes the brief last scene of the last act) to the senseless and overwhelming a measure of fate.

Fatality is one illusion live performance does well, perhaps better than recorded art, since there's never a question of special effects. Opera calls upon music, language, gesture, costume, dance, and stagecraft, to represent and project emotions across enormous spaces without additional mechanical assistance. Opera on film, opera on television, whatever its pleasures and claims upon our attention, is not what people get at the theater. There, everything has to be truly high, really good, done very well, to succeed. And operatic success, ever a rarity, receives a measure of love and adulation normally reserved for prize fetishes, and pets, and grandchildren, an inexhaustible fund of attention.

That's the aesthetic truth, but there's also a social truth about opera-going. Tickets are very dear, the taste for the form is acquired, the seats are comfortable, the audience is itself a spectacle. All who attend the opera that evening occupy a pinnacle of fortune. The opera house is the great good place. Even when, as is the case with *Wozzeck*, the characters are low, and drab, and put-upon and mad, and the scenery is slate relieved only by violence and red, the audience is nonetheless taken up to some high place where they can view the tragedy and be moved.

The 1999 Met production by Mark Lamos premiered in 1997; it completely redid the sets and staging that served Berg's opera on this stage for over 40 years, and improved upon it. Franz Grundheber sang the lead, the plain soldier Franz Wozzeck; Hildegard Behrens played Marie, the unpitied Magdalene whom he loves and murders. Dressed in military drab and cotton dowdy respectively, they act out their tragedy against a slate-colored backdrop designed by Robert Israel. James Levine conducted the Metropolitan Orchestra on this harrowing journey from oppression through degradation to extinction unredeemed by science, or social purpose, or spiritual transformation in three acts without intermission.

There is comic relief, albeit at the opera's beginning. While Wozzeck trims his Captain's hair in the first scene, the officer delivers a moral lecture to the common soldier. "You are a good man, but you lack morals. You have a child outside the sanctity of marriage." Wozzeck listens respectfully, but demurs with respect to his child. The poor man suggests that God doesn't care how a child is brought into the world, but suffers the little children... The Captain, confused by the scriptural citation, goes down on all fours and barks his displeasure at Wozzeck's reply. More relief (for us) is found in the doctor's study, in Scene 4. Wozzeck supplements his military salary by serving as a guinea pig for the regimental physician (sung by Franz Hawlata). He is required to eat only peas, and bring his urine to the Doctor for inspection. But the Doctor has seen Wozzeck pissing against the wall, like a dog. Wozzeck replies that it is only nature to seek relief, not hold it in. The Doctor's displeasure turns to rapture as Wozzeck confesses to seeing visions and hearing terrible voices, and he raises Wozzeck's salary so he may study this aberration which will make him (the Doctor) immortal. The scene ends with an order: Wozzeck, stick out your tongue.

Wozzeck's voices and visions in the open field ("It's the Freemasons!" and "A fire! A fire rising from earth to heaven...") come directly from the historical sources, but here they are sung, new music for the wounded heart. Episodes of public pleasure set in the beer garden and tavern present dancing couples who are so drunk or exhausted that they lumber around the floor leaning against each other for mutual support. When soldiers or workers sing hunting songs or drinking songs, they are atonal versions of beer hall melodies, high art versions of tunes sung by characters who can't sing on pitch. The waltzes they stumble to speak directly of Strauss and Viennese gaiety, but are skewed, artless, burdened. The guilty Marie sings a lullaby to her child by Wozzeck, about gypsies coming to steal Marie away to gypsy-land.

Act 3, Scene 2, where Wozzeck stabs Marie to death, is titled "Invention on a Single Note (B)." That note, which concludes the scene, becomes so loud and is held so long as to be unendurable—a time and place when all meanings and music converge. Why, you may ask, would anyone pay good money to participate in the unbearable? For the same reason someone would go to *Macbeth*, or *Tosca*. Because no matter how harrowing the experience of tragedy, it proves that there is another world beside the ordinary: it can make everyday life feel like a refuge.

When the cast of *Wozzeck* came back on stage to receive their well deserved bravoes after the performance, each member (still in costume) walked up to take a bow, first the supporting characters, then the principals. Hildegard Behrens, wearing the plain cotton dress of poor Marie, stepped forward as the crowd cheered and, placing her right arm across her breast so that her hand touched her left shoulder, bowed low to accept their applause. That single gesture transformed her from the underclass victim she'd become for the evening, back into the diva she is. It was a metamorphosis worthy of Ovid.

UNQUIET SOULS: *The Peony Pavilion*

The Peony Pavilion is rarer than a comet.

This classic Chinese opera written at the end of the 16th century by Tang Xianzu (who died in 1616, the same year as William Shakespeare), takes nearly twenty hours to perform when staged in entirety, as it was in New York in 1999—for the first time in centuries. The Chinese-based production was spectacular, accessible, funny, and incredibly refined. Its 55 scenes employ poetry, song, dance, acrobatics, martial arts, puppetry, and instrumental intermezzi to proclaim the primacy of love.

In his 1598 preface to the opera (as translated by Cyril Birch), Tang Xianzu wrote:

> "Love's source is unknown, yet it grows ever deeper. The living may die of it, by its power the dead live again.... Must the love that comes in a dream necessarily be unreal?...There is no lack of dream lovers in this world. Only for those whose love must be fulfilled on the pillow and for whom affection deepens only after retirement from office, is it entirely a corporeal matter...."

Sixteen-year-old Du Liniang is the only child of old Prefect Du Bao and his wife. Assigned the first poem in the *Book of Songs* by her tutor, she regrets her maidenhood. Overwhelmed by a stroll through a springtime garden, she falls asleep, and encounters a scholar-lover in a dream. She wakes up and, unable to fulfill her dream of love, eventually dies of longing. Her dreamed lover, Liu Mengmei, has also seen a beautiful girl in a garden as he slept. Unwilling to let his scholarly talents go to waste, he sets off for the capital to compete in the imperial examination that will establish his career. Travel-weary and ill, he recuperates near the tomb and shrine of Liniang. Her ghost has been given leave to return to earth by the Judge of the Underworld. She steals into Liu's room at night, where they become (again) lovers. At Liniang's command, Liu digs up her corpse, and restores it to life. The couple travels to the capital, where Liu wins the academic prize.

Meanwhile, Liniang's father has been called to defend the Southern Song Empire against a rebel attack fomented by the barbarian North. He succeeds, but is deceived into believing his wife has been killed during the disorders. Recalled to the Capital, he is made chief minister. When Liu presents himself to Du Bao as a son-in-law, the old man's rage and bitter losses prevent him from believing Liu and accepting his daughter's resurrection. The "dead" wife reappears, and in the end all are established in their proper places.

Like the unquiet souls of its protagonists, and the vexed wishes of parents and children, 13th century China where the story takes place is divided and out of harmony. The opera travels from study to garden to sickroom to shrine, from agricultural villages to besieged cities, from the court of the underworld to the court of the Southern Emperor. Du Liniang's journey through dream to death and back to life, and Liu Mengmei's quest for distinction and appointment, bring to the stage maids and scholars, monks, priests and officials, loyal servants and rebel bandits, merchants, farmers and soldiers, prostitutes and demons, a Judge of the Underworld and the offstage voice of the Emperor himself.

In Western opera, the oppositions of heart and head, family and duty, parent and child, intuition and tradition, usually resolve in triumph of one side by the other. Witness the victory of Sarastro's sages over the forces of the Queen of the Night in *The Magic Flute*, or the conflict of love and power in *Aida*. But in *The Peony Pavilion*, imbalance is the beginning, the engine of the plot. Rather than closing in a triumphal march, or sobbing over a heap of corpses, this drama travels enormous distances to attain spiritual poise.

The young Chinese director Chen Shi-Zheng, who emigrated here in 1987, brought Western notions of textual completeness and authentic performance practice to Tang Xianzu's Eastern masterpiece. Such ideas encounter inherent resistance when applied to an opera written in a performance style, *Kunju*, that has been transmitted by oral tradition. No records exist of a complete presentation of masterpiece; the archives contain no indication even how it would have been performed. The earliest instrumental musical score dates from 1792. And Chinese opera companies which carry on the Kunju tradition greeted the notion of a complete presentation with disbelief.

The theater at Laguardia Concert Hall is a curved amphitheater fronting a broad proscenium stage. For this production, two smaller platforms projected from the lip of the stage into the orchestra pit; a third, larger pavilion jutted from the center of the stage. All were built of wood using traditional carpentry and joinery. The large stage behind was open, with a Southern Song style landscape painting of water and mountains as backdrop. The wings were also open, housing tables, chairs, other properties, and costumes hung on simple pipe racks. The 12-player orchestra of flute, percussion, double reeds, strings, gongs and cymbals occupied the platform on the right, and played for all but a few moments of the epic performance. The leftmost platform served as a secondary scene of action. Most of the action took place on the central projection: its four pillars and sketch of a roof (where the caption-titles are projected in Chinese and English) suggested an interior, which became part of an open landscape by raising an arras/rear wall.

The three platforms ended in piers over a pool of water about 30 inches deep and as long as the stage is wide and lapped to within a few feet of the first row of the audience. In the pond live carp swam, with a small flock of mallards. Below the side platforms hung ten or twelve pairs of yellow finches in wooden cages. They sang throughout. This dialogue between the natural and artificial, real ducks in man-made settings, quacking and birdsong underlying singers and orchestra, subliminally informed the entire production.

Classical Chinese poetry prizes the reinflection of traditional images; elaborate rules govern the numbers of syllables in a line, the use of rhyme, and the subjects associated with forms; distinct melodies were attached to verse forms. Poems were written to old tunes (much like demotic psalms for singing), and until the 18th century, poetry served for musical notation.

The noble figures of Du Liniang, her scholar Liu Mengmei, her father the prefect Du Bao (a descendant of Du Fu, China's greatest poet) and her mother Lady Du express their heightened sensibilities through restricted forms and stylized gesture, their voices suddenly high or low, sleeves passed before the face or twirled around the hands. Every occasion, every turn of plot or encounter, has an apposite literary response, a poem or rite. The form may be artificial, but the longing, the grief, the rage, the delight, the rapture they express are direct, are piercing.

By contrast, the "low" characters including a Taoist nun and the wife of the lead bandit (both played by men), poor scholars, servants, soldiers, the outlaw rebels, barbarians, and the administrators of Hell are more natural in their movements, more vulgar in their language, and less conflicted in their appetites.

At times the line between audience and player is crossed onstage, such as when the actors applaud a sword dance or tumbler's solo. Such stagecraft may be familiar to Western theatergoers: Bertolt Brecht's plays employed placards and narrators and other illusion-shattering devices to break the dramatic bubble and turn the audience's thoughts to dialectical social criticism. Of course, the influence flowed from China to Germany: Brecht wrote his own version of the Chinese play *The Good Woman of Szechuan*.

In this opera, a silk placard announced scene changes; makeup was applied in full view; costume changes were made off to the side; puppeteers stood behind their puppets; performers applauded one another's dance and acrobatic solos (sometimes); the narrator approved of certain scenes; the search for the prize candidate began in and was carried out through the audience, then onto the stage.

Where Brecht's intention was to heighten the tension between social life and dramatic illusion in the service of a realism that was sardonic and material, the *Peony* audience and players participated in the same event, in a kind of community enchantment.

Far from sounding alien or inaccessible, the music has a real beat, and sounds akin to a Scotch-Irish southern mountain string band of banjo, fiddle and guitar, with flute and percussion added. The music of disorder, when there are barbarians, or battles, or demons about, is a structured New Year's Eve celebration played on flute and double reeds (which sound like a shawm, or bagpipes), along with gong and cymbal. In one combination or another, the orchestra plays constantly throughout the opera. In addition to supporting the dancers, coloring scenes and bridging action, it also provides sound effects and punctuates emotions. The flute often "sings" the aria along with the character.

In the world of *Peony*, love and belief are countered by authority and scepticism. When Liniang tells her story to the Tenth Judge of the Underworld, his first response is disbelief: "This is all lies. When did anyone ever die of a dream?" In Hell, there is only interrogation, and law, and punishment. Love–the source of poetry, and music, and intuition–rather than lore distinguishes the realm of the living from the land of the dead.

MUSIC ART

SPRINGTIME FOR WAGNER: *The Ring of the Nibelung*

New versions of Richard Wagner's operas are always epochal, if only because of the effort it takes to mount them. Particularly rare are productions of the complete four-opera cycle of Wagner's *Ring of the Nibelung*.

The *Ring* takes nearly twenty hours to perform. It begins underwater, travels from the caves of the underworld to Valhalla above, and ends in fire, its action spanning three generations of gods and heroes and humans. Whether measured by the demands it makes on the theater, or by the performers it requires, or by its ambition and expense, Wagner's *Ring* remains the standard for colossal music theater.

In spring of 2000, the Metropolitan Opera rolled out the first of three complete turns of Wagner's epic justifying gods' ways to man. As a fall tune-up, the Met mounted an all-new production of *Tristan und Isolde* starring Ben Heppner and Jane Eaglen, the first heroic tenor and soprano up to the task in a generation. *Tristan* has always been regarded as the purest expression of the Wagner's artistic ideal. The leads must sing their hearts out for over four hours, without benefit of action, or plot, or suspense, since everyone in the house already knows the lovers will die. (In fact, the original Tristan, Ludwig Schnorr, died of heart failure within weeks after the opera's 1865 premiere in Munich.) Their sole support, and the source of all intensity, is the orchestra, which plays without ceasing and carries them away.

Although he may not have intended to kill his first Tristan, Wagner did intend to abolish the borders between representation and experience, myth and history. He wanted his operas to be more than music, drama, poetry, or spectacle. His "art of the future" was not merely outside the usual limits of his artistic medium; it was the execution in music of the kind of thinking usually found in magnates and explorers, or conquerors and tyrants. Wagner propounded an absolute art that would enlist the sister arts in service of a transcendent form. Whatever one may think of it, his work displays a more intimate relationship with power than any other artist's, before or since.

Wagner was born in Leipzig on May 22, 1813. His mother was married to a police actuary who died shortly after his birth, and after a brief widowhood, she married Ludwig Geyer, an assimilated Jewish theatrical performer whose family had been musicians for generations. Wagner had a sound *Gymnasium* education, but received little formal musical training. And he certainly sat at the feet of no living master.

Wagner wrote his first symphony and first opera when he was nineteen, but it was in the 1840s, after a spell in Paris, that he first found real success. A string of operas—*Rienzi*, *The Flying Dutchman*, *Tannhäuser*, and *Lohengrin*—became hits, and the young lion was appointed royal music director at Dresden. Those composers who promoted his early career found themselves discarded (like Giacomo Meyerbeer, whom he rejected as an internationalist and a Jew), or exploited (like Franz Liszt, whose charisma he traded on, and whose daughter he lived with out-ofwedlock before they married).

Along the way, Wagner embraced language as no composer had before. Rather than treat the libretto as an occasion for the music, he wrote his own dramatic texts in which he invented an alliterative verse style that struck the ear as formal and slightly medieval. He fashioned a mythology out of Norse and Celtic myth that felt meaningful and allegorical (which is not to say explicable). Here was an unexplored musical continent of gods, dragons, dwarves, and heroes, haunted by recurrent strains and dissonances, lapped by alien seas. It wasn't just new opera; it was a new form of art.

This new art required a new building to house it, and the ideal auditorium Wagner finally succeeded in building in Bayreuth represented a complete departure from previous custom. The audience all faced forward toward the raised stage in a darkened house (as moviegoers do), with the orchestra concealed in a pit below the level of the stage. This was not a ballroom, where the performance was incidental, or a curved opera house, where the audience gazed across the orchestra at one another. Wagner transformed the music theater of bourgeois Western Europe into a church of the emotions. His operas, as Charles Baudelaire put it, had the same effect as drugs.

But Baudelaire was thinking of its private, individual effect, and German music had a national mission. According to Wagner, the Romantic impulse in poetry had turned away from the heroic to the æsthetic, inward, and decadent. He believed that even Johann Wolfgang Goethe, the seminal figure of German Romanticism, could not bear to represent the true condition of the human spirit. The voice of individual striving could not resist the "practical plurality of everyday occurrences," Wagner wrote. "The romance poem turned into Journalism." And thus "the poet's art has turned to politics: No one now can poetize, without politicizing."

Wagner's artistic ideal was instead the representation of feeling so powerful that the beholder "passes into that ecstatic state where one forgets the fateful question 'Why?'" Rather than being accountable, civilized, and sensible, his art would move the human spirit out from under labor and frustration, and suspend it in a realm that gratifies and redeems. It was to this end that he deployed all the artistic means at his disposal—mythology, poetry, drama, spectacle, symphonic orchestra, even architecture—to imply some kind of new human being and new world order.

A great deal of ink has been spilled trying to explain just what Wagner's *Ring* is about. Wagner himself thought the operas sang the origin of the German national spirit in the legends of pre-Christian Europe. (The Nazis and other nationalist mystagogues made much of this same source.) But George Bernard Shaw, remembering Wagner's youth on the revolutionary barricades of Dresden, interpreted the gods of Valhalla as proto-capitalists and the dwarves (who actually build the castles and forge the weapons) as the despised workers. Musicologist Richard Taruskin makes a witty case for the *Ring* as an allegory of godlike composers giving laws to the performers, whose glory consists in the faithful realization of their masters' intentions.

A *précis* hardly does justice to the complexity and recalcitrance of Wagner's libretto for the *Ring*. Much of the mythical strength of the narrative comes from its refusal to be reduced to an explanation—but then, mystic incomprehensibility has always enjoyed a long run.

In *Das Rheingold*, Alberich of the Nibelung (a tribe of dwarves who inhabit the underground realm of Nibelhelm) renounces love, which is the magical requirement for anyone who wants to steal the gold of the nymphatic Rhine maidens. Meanwhile, up in the heavens, Wotan is trying to weasel out of his promise to give his sister-in-law Freia, goddess of youth and beauty, in payment to the giants Fafner and Fasolt for building Valhalla, the hall of the gods. But the crafty god Loge has a plan. He suggests to Wotan that they give the giants as substitute payment the treasures a dwarf named Mime has forged for Alberich from the Rhinegold: the Ring of Power and the Tarnhelm (a helmet that allows whoever wears it to assume any shape). So Wotan and Loge descend and trick Alberich out of the Ring and Tarnhelm, which they swap for Freia. Alberich curses whoever possesses the Ring. Fafner kills Fasolt. The gods cross the rainbow bridge back to Valhalla, ignoring the pleas of the Rhine maidens to return their stolen gold.

In *Die Walküre*, Siegmund, the mortal son of Wotan, finds himself in the house of Hunding, his enemy. Hunding's wife Sieglinde falls in love with Siegmund. She tells about a sword a stranger plunged into a tree that only her long-lost brother can remove. Siegmund removes it. The lovers discover they are brother and sister. Wotan orders the Valkyrie Brünnhilde to protect his son from Hunding, but Fricka, Wotan's wife, insists that the marriage bonds be defended. Caught between law and will, Wotan at last decides for law and orders Brünnhilde to aid Hunding. She defies him, but Siegmund is slain anyway, though the pregnant Sieglinde escapes with the (now broken) sword. Sieglinde shelters near Fafner's cave. Brünnhilde is sentenced to become a mortal and sleep, surrounded by a wall of fire, until awakened by a mortal hero.

In *Siegfried*, the hero Siegfried, reared by the dwarf Mime after his mother Sieglinde's death, knows no fear. At Mime's forge, he remakes his father's broken sword. Mime sees the youth as a way to gain the Ring. Wotan warns Alberich against Mime, and both try to rouse Fafner (now a dragon thanks to the Tarnhelm's magic) and urge him to return the Ring to the Rhine maidens. Siegfried kills Fafner and claims the Ring. Tasting dragon's blood, he understands the language of the forest birds, who tell him that Mime is plotting against him. The hero kills Mime. The birds also tell him of a maiden asleep on a rock, circled by fire. Siegfried meets Wotan at a crossroads, and shatters the god's spear. Siegfried wakes Brünnhilde. They love.

In *Götterdämmerung*, the Germanic Fates, the Norns, predict the fall of the gods. Siegfried takes leave of Brünnhilde. He gives her the Ring of the Nibelungs, and she gives him her horse. Hagen, son of Loge and half-brother of Gunther, Lord of the Gibichungs, counsels his brother to marry Brünnhilde. They drug Siegfried into forgetfulness, and marry him to Gutrune, Gunther's sister. The hero agrees to bring Brünnhilde to Gunther. A Valkyrie begs Brünnhilde to return the Ring to the Rhine maidens. She refuses. Siegfried assumes Gunther's shape, and claims both bride and Ring. Brünnhilde wants revenge. She joins with Hagen and Gunther in a plot to murder Siegfried. On the banks of the Rhine, Siegfried is stabbed in the back. He remembers Brünnhilde and dies. Hagen kills Gunther, and Brünnhilde rushes into Siegfried's funeral pyre. The Rhine overflows, the Rhine maidens drown Hagen and regain their gold, and Valhalla burns. Only our world remains.

The entire run of the Metropolitan Opera's fall production of *Tristan* was sold out. As the first new Tristan and Isolde in many years, Ben Heppner and Jane Eaglen, and the orchestra directed by James Levine, performed to a high standard. The stage was bare, the performers backlit as they sang in tableaux for four full hours.

Tristan und Isolde promised great things for spring's coming *Ring*. But not entirely. In Act One of *Tristan*, as the lovers drank their potion, the stage lighting shifted color and an audible minority in the audience—which would have been receiving erotic communion at this moment a hundred years ago—tittered. Audiences have always been divided into Wagnerites and non-Wagnerites, and going to one of his operas has always been like attending a political rally: thrilling for the party members, chilling for the poor stray who wanders in.

But the giggling at *Tristan und Isolde* derived from another source. The opera begins after the fact, when all that remains is to declare and die. There are no seductions, no compromises. All that remains is the composer's relentless pursuit of the power of his "art of the future." Some deem it unfair to blame Wagner for Hitler, who adopted both Beethoven's music and Wagner's "art of the future" for the sound-track and storyline of the Third Reich. But surely it is fair to point out that Wagner's characters do not live in the sense that Shakespeare's Hamlet lives, or Goethe's Faust, or even Alban Berg's

Wozzeck. Tristan, Isolde, and the characters of the *Ring*, are as powerful a creation as any artist has ever managed—but they are incomplete as creatures. They do not live outside the music.

Even moved by the music, the characters of the art of the future are doomed victims. This, rather than rabid anti-Semitism, is the origin of the composer's appeal to 20th-century tyrants. It beguiled Hitler, and prompted Stalin to command a production of *Die Walküre* at the Bolshoi theater just before the outbreak of the Second World War. Wagner's impact on an audience—his concentration of every available resource toward a single effect—suits the totalitarian, who also wants to sway crowds and topple monuments. The future has always provided a convenient justification to those who regard themselves as new and powerful, with nothing to restrain them.

As the despot is to the state, so Wagner is to his created world. Hitler and Stalin are like bad artists, who regard people as incomplete beings waiting to be played upon and animated by their masters. Wagner is a great artist, great enough to understand that his heroes must be incomplete, and flawed, and lacking. Hitler's Aryans, his genetic ideal, had no flaws. Like his gods and heroes and dwarves, Wagner's art of the future becomes merely an instrument when placed in the hands of the state.

Power in politics and in art must destroy the imagination by denying that there is any alternative to its single purpose, its directed version of the future. The *Ring of the Nibelung*, though fed by a wellspring of the spirit, presents life without hope except annihilation. It is an enclosed world of sound and shadows on the wall. On the other side of the wall, out of earshot, is where people can actually live.

CHEWING GUM: *American Poetry: The Twentieth Century*

In 1861, Francis Turner Palgrave helped define Victorian taste by publishing *The Golden Treasury*, "a true national Anthology of three centuries" of British poetry that contained not a single work by William Blake, Christopher Smart, or John Donne. In 1874, Palgrave's American friend Ralph Waldo Emerson published an anthology of American poetry that left out Walt Whitman and Edgar Allan Poe. It's most often in their omissions that anthologies of poetry grow interesting—for it's in the omissions that you can measure the risks the editor is willing to take.

So what are we to make of the first two volumes of *American Poetry: The Twentieth Century*, issued this millennial year by the prestigious Library of America? Perhaps the reader can set aside the fact that the volumes contain no statement about the selection process, though that's a very bad sign. And perhaps the reader can set aside the fact that their title pages do not name anyone as the editor of record, which is an even worse sign. (A five-member advisory board is listed in the front matter, but no clue is given as to whom they are advising.) But that still leaves us faced with the fact that these volumes seem determined to omit almost nothing.

Presenting the poets chronologically by date of birth, *American Poetry: The Twentieth Century* opens with Henry Adams, born in 1838. Nearly two thousand pages later, the march of poetry calls a temporary halt at May Swenson, born in 1919. Given the postwar population boom and the massive increase in published poetry after 1950, the Library of America is looking at a journey of ten thousand pages to complete its work. This is not anthologizing, but a riskless attempt at unedited inclusiveness. It's like reprinting a hundred years' worth of newspapers and calling what you're doing the writing of history.

This new collection follows upon the Library of America's *American Poetry: The Nineteenth Century*. That fine two-volume work, published in 1993, actually has a named editor in John Hollander, who presents American poets from Philip Freneau (1752-1832) through Trumbull Stickney (1874-1904) in order of birth. Hollander's notes include a masterful thumbnail biography of each poet, and a time-line chronology clarifies the relations among the writers and their time.

Trading on the authority of its predecessor, the first two volumes of *American Poetry: The Twentieth Century* announce on their dustjackets that they embrace "nearly 1,400 poems by over 200 poets...in a series that will ultimately survey the entire century."

But what is a twentieth-century poem? And who is a twentieth-century poet? Henry Adams (better known as an historian, journalist, novelist, and Brahmin), Lizette Woodworth Reese (1856-1935), Harriet Monroe (1860-1936, the founder of *Poetry* magazine, which launched Ezra Pound and modernism in America), the novelist Edith Wharton (1862-1937), and Edward Arlington Robinson (1869-1935) appear in both the nineteenth- and twentieth-century anthologies. Why these five and not, for example, the philosopher George Santayana (1863-1952)? (Though here, at least, one does find someone omitted from this endless anthology.)

Henry Adams's "Prayer to the Virgin of Chartres" follows five anonymous ballads as the first signed work in the collection. Adams once remarked in a letter that "all the notices from today to doomsday will never make an American public care for poetry—or anything else unless perhaps chewing gum."

Lindley Williams Hubbell (1901-1994) in "Beer Bottles" observes: There are more poems in the world/ Than empty beer bottles/ So many millions of poems have been written!/ What happens to them all? Who reads them all?

In "Poetry," Marianne Moore (1887-1972) again sounds poetry's dissonant chord about itself: I, too, dislike it: there are things that are important beyond all this fiddle./ Reading it, however, with a perfect contempt for it, one discovers in/ it after all, a place for the genuine.

We have, as Moore points out, a real need for the genuine in poetry, and it's possible to learn from these volumes of twentieth-century poetry the difference between the genuine and the contrived. But that's not because all the work here is genuine poetry.

In fact, the all-inclusiveness of *American Poetry: The Twentieth Century* does give us something, for it suggests the possibility of distinguishing four orders of descending importance in twentieth-century American verse.

Among writers born through 1919, the canon of major poets remains pretty much what it has been for the last forty or fifty years: Ezra Pound (1885-1972) and T.S. Eliot (1888-1965), Robert Frost (1874-1963) and Wallace Stevens (1879-1955), Marianne Moore and William Carlos Williams (1883-1963), Hart Crane (1899-1932), e.e. cummings (1894-1962), Elizabeth

Bishop (1911-1979), Theodore Roethke (1908-1963), and Langston Hughes (1902-1967).

Major poets write poems of the first order. They have a sizable body of work. What makes their poetry of the first order is that their poems contain complete thoughts, and each poem is a new thought. Read Frost's "Provide, Provide," or Stevens's "The Man on the Dump," for good examples. Or Marianne Moore's "Is Your Town Nineveh":

Why so desolate?
    in phantasmagoria about fishes,
        what disgusts you? Could
            not all personal upheaval in
                the name of freedom, be tabooed?

Is it Nineveh
    and are you Jonah
        in the sweltering east wind of your wishes?
        I myself, have stood
            there by the aquarium, looking
                at the Statue of Liberty.

Some poetry of the first order is written by less familiar poets, such as Robert Francis (1901-1987), in "By Night":

After midnight I heard a scream.
    I was awake. It was no dream.
But whether it was bird of prey
Or prey of bird I could not say.
I never heard that sound by day.

MUSIC ART

Sometimes work of the first order is produced by those whose poetry is a background activity, such as Henry Adams. Marsden Hartley (1877-1943) is best remembered as a painter, but his poem "Fishmonger" is so electric, it makes this anthology look like a good idea:

> I have taken scales from off
> The cheeks of the moon.
> I have made fins from bluejays' wings,
> I have made eyes from damsons in the shadow.
> I have taken flushes from the peachlips in the sun,
> From all these I have made a fish of heaven for you,
> Set it swimming on a young October sky.
> I sit on the bank of the stream and watch
> The grasses in amazement
> As they turn to ashy gold.
> Are the fishes from the rainbow
> Still beautiful to you,
> For whom they are made,
> For whom I have set them,
> Swimming?

Poetry of the second order, however, articulates a familiar thought, or the same set of ideas over and over: time's passage, for instance, or the sting of injustice, the beauty of nature, love and desire, cruelty and yearning. Here are poetry's Great Plains, spacious and crossed by many; here is the home of the middle class; here one can make a life.

Poets of the second order (which is the largest party of poets in the collection) are skilled and accessible. Edward Arlington Robinson, Dorothy Parker (1893-1967), Kenneth Rexroth (1905-1982), and Edna St. Vincent Millay (1892-1950) are strong in single poems, but are difficult to stay with. Their problem is eventual monotony.

The third order of poetry may have no ideas at all. It can embody a sensibility, make gestures, proceed by method, or stand in opposition. Gertrude Stein's (1874-1946) "Stanzas in Meditation" and John Cage's (1912-1992) experiments with chance and arbitrary arrangement are higher forms of this art. Its lesser practitioners can start out amusing and end up unreadable. Here, for instance, are some lines from Abraham Lincoln Gillespie's (1895-1950) "A Purplexicon of Dissynthegrations": punziplaze karmasokist DecoYen Pompieraeian/ scaruscatracery timmedigets outrége Opinducts. And this goes on for another fifty-nine lines. A less metaphysical essay is Elsa von Freytag-Loringhoven's (1874-1927) "Klink—Hratzvenga (Deathwail)," which begins: Ildrich mitzdonja—astatootch/ Ninj—iffe kniek—/ Ninj—iffe kniek!

The fourth and final order of poetry included in *American Poetry: The Twentieth Century* are works that appear for social reasons. This accounts for contributions by Walter Conrad Arensberg (1878-1954, patron of the avant garde), John Reed (1887-1920, author of *Ten Days That Shook the World*), the novelist John Dos Passos (1896-1970), the critics R.P. Blackmur (1904-1965), Yvor Winters (1900-1968), and Edmund Wilson (1895-1972), the social philosopher Paul Goodman (1911-1972), and the playwright Tennessee Williams (1911-1983).

This anthology also contains a number of show tunes, folk songs, and blues lyrics. These are not poems. It's impossible for anyone to read an Oscar Hammerstein II (1895-1960) lyric, and not hear the music the words were written to and with and for. Just look at "Ole Man River" as it sits on the page. Poetry may embrace democracy, but it sure isn't democratic. It no more includes the lyrics of W.C. Handy (1873-1958), Ma Rainey (1886-1939), Charley Patton (1887-1934), Irving Berlin (1888-1989), Bessie Smith (1898-1937), Lorenz Hart (1895-1943), Ira Gershwin (1896-1983), E.Y. Harburg (1896-1981), Blind Lemon Jefferson (1897-1929), Bukka White (1909-1977), or Frank Loesser (1910-1969), say, than the Mosaic Law includes the Motor Vehicle code.

The difference is that poetry, no matter what outward form it assumes, has its own music. Samuel Taylor Coleridge talks about an even distribution of tone throughout the work, which gives rise to a living voice, recognizable even in the middle of the desert; John Ashbery calls it the magnetizing of language. Poems are written and sit on the page. They wait for the reader as the printed score waits for the soloist, or the conductor, to be realized. If the reader can hear a living voice addressing him, in a way he can attend to and understand, then he has performed the poem and animated its voice.

A song lyric, on the other hand, comes with a melody. Try to read Dorothy Fields's "I Can't Give You Anything but Love" as it is punctuated in these pages and not as it is sung. Who can value a transcription of a blues song when the original is out there, accessible, and probably better known than most of the poems in this anthology?

Generally speaking, poetry doesn't sell well in the bookstores. So it's one of those oddities of the marketplace that publishers call stuff poetry in order to sell it. It's as though the compilers of this anthology, by importing ringers from other genres, have attempted a little reverse marketing. But poetry is not a commodity. It is the publisher's bad conscience.

Reading this anthology, one begins to wonder what "American poetry" means. Is it written by citizens of the United States, either native or naturalized? Is it poetry written here, no matter what the legal status of the poet? Is it poetry that takes American places, people, and speech for its matter, but is written anywhere? Is it poetry written in American English? Can a person renounce being American, the way someone can choose to be American?

These are questions *American Poetry: The Twentieth Century* resolutely refuses to answer. You'll find here all the expected poems by the American expatriates. And you'll find as well poems by Elsa von Freytag-Loringhoven, Helen Adam (who writes poems in Scots dialect), and Vladimir Nabokov—works that are American only because they were written in America. (I'm not suggesting these shouldn't be included, but I am curious to see how the series eventually will rule on W. H. Auden, Joseph Brodsky, and Paul Muldoon.)

The two long-standing traditions in poetry in English are the plain style and the golden. Of the twentieth century's major poets, T.S.

Eliot and Robert Frost practice plain style. This tends to be direct, apparently unadorned, and sober. The voice is not distanced, and addresses the reader directly.

The golden style employs tropes and rhetoric, elaborate wit, is often self-conscious and referential, relying upon literary fancy rather than plain speech and moral order. The golden style is more playful, while the plain style appears more earnest. When Ezra Pound characterized T.S. Eliot as preferring Moses to the Muses, this is what he meant. The plain-style Frost and golden-style Stevens never tempered their mutual rivalry and mistrust. In his poems, Stevens always referred to himself in the third person.

But there's another dichotomy. Frost and Stevens are eminently American poets. They lived in America, they wrote about the place and spoke its language. (Frost did launch his career in England, but only as a strategy to get his due back home.) Stevens didn't leave the country at all, except for vacations in the Caribbean; he kept up on art and philosophy through books, journals, and catalogs. Neither one of them shared in the glamour accorded the tribe of American expatriates active in Europe before World War II.

Pound and Eliot left America for the Old World with the explicit intention of promulgating what Pound called "World Literature." Following Dante's light as Dante followed Virgil's, Eliot became a British citizen and returned here only for lecture tours and other public occasions. His poetry conjures unreal cities and imaginary landscapes, an alien and eternal anywhere:

> Under a juniper-tree the bones sang, scattered and shining
> We are glad to be scattered, we did little good to each other,

> Under a tree in the cool of the day, with the blessing of sand,
> Forgetting themselves and each other, united
> In the quiet of the desert. This is the land which ye
> Shall divide by lot. And neither division nor unity
> Matter. This is the land. We have our inheritance.

Pound, whose strongest poetry now appears to be the translations and imitations he wrote before 1920, invented a world of bards and troubadours, sages and scholar poets, truth-telling historians and displaced persons, which he inhabited as a man without a country. The early poems are so good, and Pound's social shadow so long and deep, that he cannot be disappeared from any history of poetry, no matter how disagreeable his politics, how poisonous his rage. And Pound, like Eliot, thought of what he did as world poetry rather than American. In his "perfect" Canto XIII, Pound's Chinese sage Kung (that's Confucius) recalls

> A day when the historians left blanks in their writings,
> I mean for things they didn't know,
> But that time seems to be passing.

EYE ALTERING: *William Blake*

William Blake (1757-1827) is the prophet of contraries. According to his wife Catherine, he lived much of his time in Paradise.

William Blake, the 2001 exhibition at the Metropolitan Museum of Art in New York, was a scaled-back version of the Blake retrospective at London's Tate Gallery detailed in the printed catalogue. The show gathered in one place works that most people only have known by report, or by reputation, or in reproduction. The actual things were, and are, an eyeful, and a mindful, and a soulful.

With a justice perhaps tempered by lack of recognition, Blake regarded John Milton and William Shakespeare as his peers in English poetry. As an artist, he claimed fellowship with Albrecht Dürer and Michelangelo. His prophetic familiars were Isaiah and Ezekiel. The technique he invented for engraving his illuminated books as described in *The Marriage of Heaven and Hell* was a gift from the infernal regions. Blake the poet often talked with angels, and printers have historically employed devils. Gutenberg's business partner was Johannes Faust.

A bronze head of William Blake cast from a life mask made in the artist's sixties ushered visitors in and out of the Met exhibit. Just to the right, in the section "One of the Gothic Artists," hung a large engraving from about 1820, titled *The Laocoön as Jehovah with Satan and Adam*. It serves as an emblem and capable figure of Blake's intent. Blake filled the entire background of this Homeric cartoon of the Trojan prophet and his sons devoured by a serpent with rubrics, and dicta, and glosses. "Where any view of Money exists," he proclaims across the top, "Art cannot be carried on, but War." The large caption across the bottom of the engraving reads "YH [in Hebrew characters] & his two Sons Satan & Adam as they were copied from the Cherubim of Solomon's Temple by three Rhodians & applied to Natural Fact or History of Ilium."

For Blake, the true and authentic was Hebraic, or Celtic, or Gothic: the pre-existing, the suppressed, concealed, chthonic, denied. Classicism, the making of art and poetry after Greek and Roman models, enslaves imagination.

The Metropolitan retrospective chronicled Blake's lifelong mental fight against the mind-forged manacles: engravings the commercial artist made to illustrate works of other writers (his bread and butter); sketches, drawings and paintings in pencil, ink, watercolor and tempera; illuminated books of his writings integrated with images and designs of his own devise; and large-scale prints without text that combine the engraver's with the painter's art.

There was also Blake's copy of *Paradise Lost*, and his annotated edition of Sir Joshua Reynolds's *Discourses*. Blake has written on the title page: "This Man was Hired to Depress Art." A bespectacled Sir Joshua gazes blandly back at the reader from the facing page.

Blake justified his resentment of the academic and social oil painters of his generation such as Reynolds and William Gainsborough on both artistic and commercial grounds. Artistically, oil painting could be reworked and overlaid, concealing all but the final effect. Blake advocated truth in line—painting is drawing with color; and truth in material—tempera, watercolor and ink accurately record the creative hand. In the marketplace, bad art corrupts public taste and, like bad money, drives out the good.

Blake didn't set out to be poor, or to be overlooked. In the 1790s and first years of the 19th century, he developed a unique method for producing printed works that combined word and image on a single copper plate. The results of those technical and imaginative experiments were offered to the public at large through prospectus and in the equivalent of a private gallery at his print shop in the Hercules Building, Lambeth. He found fewer takers then than there were viewers at the press preview of this exhibition.

Thanks to the scope and quality of this museum show, I could compare Blake's actual creations to the increasingly detailed and crisp reproductions of his handiwork available both in the lavish catalogue that accompanies the exhibition, and in a noble series of facsimile illuminated books published by Princeton University Press in seven volumes. Although mechanical reproduction was part of Blake's process, there's a universe of difference between his pages and the pictures of his pages on a page.

Blake's method for producing works which unified word and image as a single act of imagination is both technical and artistic. Inspired by a dream-communication from his dead brother Robert, William developed a method of drawing and writing in an acid-resistant liquid on copper plate, so that his lines would be raised when the background was etched away by acid.

Blake learned to write legibly and backwards in his acid-resist ink, a calligraphic feat that probably requires a Koranic scribe or master of the Chinese brush to fully appreciate. After etched plates were finished, Blake could take his pages to press. To make an edition of *Songs of Innocence*, each plate was inked, then impressed on wet paper. After the impression dried, Blake added watercolor by hand. In later experiments, he used several colored inks, sometimes in several stages. Each impression was unique. The state of the copper plate altered from edition to edition, and each application of watercolors was freshly improvised within the context of the page.

The illuminated books are mechanically assisted art, rather than mechanically reproduced works of art, or printing. There, imagination lives in the material. Digitized color printing, faithful though it may be to the outward appearance of Blake's pages, can only apply ink on the surface of the paper, and only repeat what exists already. In letterpress, ink pushes through the surface, and marries the paper. Chance and spirit supply the rest.

Innocence and *Experience*, when hung on the wall as they were in this exhibition, turn into something other than books. A page read as a poster is not the same as a page in a book. By the same ratio, the experience of a poem is one thing when read in its illuminated printer's Eden, and another and more common event when encountered in exile, on the text-only page of Blake's *Complete Writings*. These losses and redemptions are not restricted to museums or to reading rooms.

Other pleasures and illuminations at this exhibition couldn't be contained within the pages of a book, such as the chance to occupy the same room as some of William Blake's large scale (21"x30") color prints like *Pity*, and *Newton*, and *Nebuchadnezzar*, and the color-printed relief etching *God Judging Adam*. The artist called them "frescos," meaning the images were intended for walls, albeit portable.

The Met displayed two generations of *God Judging Adam*. In one version God and Adam, Maker and Image, appear as warm-tinted figures against a misty heaven. To its right, the Creator and his Image are depicted as pale, cool-fleshed beings, in heightened contrast to the darkened earth and God's chariot of fire. The serial states of these prints do not read like variations on a theme. Instead, they present a revelation of latent meaning, of the hidden, through successive impressions, a series of animation cels in a feature of invisible content.

Blake's pen and watercolor illustrations of John Milton's *Paradise Lost* possess an accuracy that can only be attributed to Blake's power as a reader, or to the direct inspiration the artist received when Milton descended from heaven in the form of a comet and entered Blake's left foot, as depicted in plate 29 of *Milton a Poem*.

The finished state of these paintings is striking when compared to the series of sketches and illustrations for an edition of Dante's *Divine Comedy* that Blake was in the process of planning and realizing at the end of his life. Where Milton's Chaos and Heaven and Hell were part of Blake's vision of elemental creation and so could be realized in full detail, Dante followed Virgil. The hierarchic, architected heaven and hell and in-between must have repelled Blake, even as the music of the Florentine's demotic epic must have attracted him.

Blake's earlier thoughts about Dante can be traced in his 1803 tempera and ink portrait of the poet of exile, painted around the same time and in the same format as his portrait of Milton.

The long-haired poet wears a Puritan collar, his sightless eyes facing the viewer. An oak wreath circles Milton's head, a medallion set against the green background. The serpent with apple occupies the ground, slithering behind the poet from right to left. An epic poet's lyre frames the left side of the picture; on the right stands a pastoral oaten pipe.

Blake portrays Dante Alighieri in prison. The exile wears a scholar's hood, and is framed by the laureate's wreath denied him by his native Florence. A heavy chain attached to a stone wall occupies the left side of the composition. Dante faces right, where Count Ugolino and his sons (*Inferno* XXXIII) await the inevitable cannibal horror.

The poet of contrary states, who celebrated impulse and decried moralizing, understood that appetite had a dark side, but wasn't glum about it. *The Ghost of a Flea*–done in tempera and gold leaf on a mahogany panel–depicts the spiritual apparition of a Flea that visited the artist in the last decade of his life. According to his friend John Varley, who was present at the time, the vision told Blake that "all fleas were inhabited by the souls of such men, as were by nature bloodthirsty to excess, and were therefore providentially confined to the size and form of insects..."

In Blake's Paradise, the contraries cease striving with each other. His poem "Auguries of Innocence" from a manuscript of about 1803 is an agemate of the frescoes without words. It accomplishes in verse what his fresco *Nebuchadnezzar* does in line and color, simultaneously compelling the opposites to be visible and remain there, for as long as one can bear to look:

> Every Night & every Morn
> Some to Misery are Born.
> Every Morn & every Night
> Some are born to sweet delight.
> Some are Born to sweet delight,
> Some are Born to Endless Night.
> We are led to Believe a Lie
> When we see not Thro' the Eye
> Which was Born in a Night to perish in a Night
> When the Soul Slept in Beams of Light.
> God Appears & God is Light
> To those poor Souls who dwell in Night,
> But does a Human Form Display
> To those who Dwell in Realms of day.

Other mystics have brought tidings of the spiritual world that is located alongside, inside, above or behind the physical realm. Cabalists and alchemists, ecstatics and enthusiasts express themselves through recondite symbols, and articulated systems, in parables and legends. They speak to the initiated, or draw blanks. William Blake is akin to the mystagogues, but he speaks of the eternal in a language of such specificity, charm and gravity that anyone, innocent or experienced, must stop and listen.

With Shakespeare and perhaps Milton, Blake is his own place, and like no other. William Shakespeare's medium was primarily theatrical, the world we see and those who live in it his theme. Cosmopolitan John Milton read all the books, knew all the learned languages and sciences, served as Oliver Cromwell's Latin Secretary, and wrote to justify God's ways to man. William Blake, London printer, draftsman and autodidact, employed his skills to depict an eternal mental war as yet in progress, and largely unremarked. Shakespeare wrote the present, Milton's subject (loss of Eden) is what's past. Blake makes visible the prospect of redemption and rebuilt Jerusalem.

No other major artist or poet leaves so little room for comfort as William Blake. Many who admire his songs often feel compelled to dismiss the prophetic books as madness—I suppose to maintain their urbanity. Those who read the prophecies in order to explain them, even brave and true souls like Northrop Frye, end up trying to fasten mercury with a tack. Blake's cosmology looks something like the Kabbalah; his version of the physical resembles alchemy (an art which Newton practiced); his drawings and paintings are indeed the equals of Dürer and Michelangelo. But his very scope seems to undermine his authority, just as his imaginative power and directness of expression subvert not his vision, but his audience: How is it possible to see so clearly that which can't be seen? How can a person know what this person testifies to so unmistakably? It's not the stuff of journalism and current events. Blake's is truly news that stays news, or will be.

Prophecy does not illuminate God, who needs no illuminating, or the prophet, who is the means not the end. Prophetic works illuminate the reader, the witness, those who can hear what they can bear, and are changed for the experience. I never thought that I understood Blake's prophetic poems as a whole, any more than I understand *Ezekiel* or

Isaiah. But there are moments in all those books whose meaning is clear. Take these lines from *Jerusalem*, Plate 91:

> I have tried to make friends by corporeal gifts but have only
> Made enemies: I never made friends but by spiritual gifts;
> By severe contentions of friendship & the burning fire of thought.

or later, at the bottom of the same page:

> I care not whether a Man is Good or Evil; all that I care
> Is whether he is a Wise Man or a Fool.

Almost alone among artists, Blake's work bears direct testimony to the dealings between man as he actually lives, and a God people still believe in. His poetry doesn't play upon tellings or retellings of the received truth; instead, it plays a vision and music descended from the Hebrew prophets, sung in a different country, at a later moment in eternity.

I'm not certain which is the plate and which the impression, but I am convinced that William Blake's craggy prophecies are proofs of the limpid *Songs of Innocence and Experience*. Like the successive states of his frescos *God Judging Adam* and *Pity*, every encounter with the poems teases more of what was latent into sight.

I turn again to the infinite argument of his engraved *Laocoön*. There the poet/prophet proclaims that "The Eternal Body of Man is The Imagination, that is God himself The Divine Body/ It manifests itself in his Works of Art (In Eternity All is Vision)." Just reading these things can be thrilling and perplexing. To see them in the flesh is to visit the land of strong conviction.

MUSIC ART

INTO EGYPT: Along the Nile

On September 10, 2001, the day before we were attacked, I attended a press preview for two small photography exhibitions devoted to Egypt at the Metropolitan Museum in New York. "Along the Nile," a show mounted by the photography department, featured photographs of Egypt made in the 1850s and 1860s. The other, "The Pharaoh's Photographer," presented stills and silent-movie footage by the Met's own archæological photo-documentarian, Harry Burton. Once the museum reopened, both shows ran through the end of December.

Every photograph takes the past as its subject—and turns that subject into an object. And like a photograph, the past is two-dimensional. In one way, ancient Egypt exists in the same plane, the same uniform and intelligible past, as the Declaration of Independence, or Omaha Beach, or the day before yesterday. But in another way, ancient Egypt exists in an entirely other place—broken off from us, unintelligible: Its gods had animal heads, its magicians were the most powerful, its writing was pictures. Countless slaves toiled to raise monuments to their incestuous masters in the Valley of the Kings.

Maxime Du Camp was a nineteenth-century French journalist and photographer. The son-in-law of Jean François Champollion, the discoverer of the Rosetta Stone, Du Camp made this first photo-documentary tour of the ruins of ancient Egypt in the company of his young friend, the novelist Gustave Flaubert. While the novelist sampled Oriental sensation, the journalist recorded images of the temple at Abu Simbel (at a site now submerged by the waters behind the Aswan dam), the Sphinx (half-buried, its nose defaced by a Napoleonic cannonball), the Pyramids, Amenhotep's Colossus and the Tomb of Ozymandias (he of Shelley's poem: Look on my works, ye mighty, and despair).

The photographic prints themselves possess the uncanny patina of old objects. These pictures also look eerie also because they are empty, no people at all save for the lone figure of Du Camp's assistant posed beside a column, or at the base of a statue, to establish scale. It may be that pre-tourist Egypt didn't have much in the way of everyday activity around its monuments. Or perhaps the photographer chose a quiet time to shoot. Or the vacancy may be a side-effect of technology: Anything that moves would not appear at all, or would only leave the ghost of an image on the paper negative's necessarily long exposure. The one picture Du Camp did take of a camera-shy Flaubert in a Cairo back-street wearing native dress relies on its caption to declare its meaning. It could be a picture of anyone.

Those European and American photographers who followed Du Camp into Egypt—George Wilson Bridges, Félix Teynard, John Beasley Greene, Ernest Benecke, Théodule Devéria, Gustav Le Gray—either found new subjects or new takes on now standard motifs. The German Benecke's portraits of Egyptian musicians, of two dancing girls, of a master and two slaves in Cairo, and his photograph of an autopsy of a crocodile, have that posed frozen quality and grainy focus that makes old prints look more like art objects than like documentation. An early example of society photography, Le Gray's 1867 photograph of the shipboard fete for His Highness Ismail Pasha makes the occasion look even duller than it must have been.

When photographers migrated from paper to glass negatives in the 1850s, they were able to produce sharper pictures with shorter exposures. Félix Bonfils and Francis Frith worked with the newer technology. Their photographs have a clarity that immediately distinguishes them from their predecessors. An example of contemporary state-of-the-art imaging, Frith's stereo view of the Chapel of Ramesses II, displayed in a stereopticon rather than on the wall as a print, is every bit as arresting in the context of this two-room gallery exhibit as it must have been when it was first published around 1860. On the documentary side, Bonfils' picture of the Temple of Dendur clearly shows the actual condition and site of a monumental structure that now resides inside its own glass pyramid pavilion at the Metropolitan Museum, just down the hall from the Galleries of Egyptian Art, where "The Pharaoh's Photographer" is hung.

From 1919 until his death in 1940, Harry Burton documented the epic excavations conducted by the Met Egyptologist Howard Carter and his British patron Lord Carnarvon in the Nile valley. Part of Burton's job was to catalogue all the finds of the expedition, both in the place of their discovery, and again after being removed to the collection. Additionally, Burton recorded the events of the dig, most famously the unearthing and opening of Tutankhamon's Tomb.

Burton's are archives with a difference. His subjects have historic, dramatic, and scholarly interest. His photography, straightforward and transparent, lets the people, events and things speak through them. Exposed on glass negatives, using some artificial but primarily reflected available light, his photographs of tomb interiors show the storerooms to be more like high-end attics or curiosity shops than awe-inspiring displays. In some pictures, the objects have been tagged with identification numbers before being moved. In a time-lapse study, four images made in 1936 record the complete unwrapping of a mummy, a long-standing mystery revealed.

Burton also took pictures of people, of native bearers in the procession of objects taken from the Tomb, of Howard Carter looking through the open doors of Tut's second shrine, of tourists and curiosity seekers to a site that has inspired countless romances and scary movies.

The Hollywood connection is more than speculative. Met Museum trustee Edward S. Harkness purchased a hand-cranked movie camera for the Egyptian expedition in 1921. The new equipment made it to Luxor in 1922, and Burton taught himself how to work the machine. The expedition acquired a second camera the following year, and in 1924 the museum photographer went to Hollywood to study film lighting. It's plain that someone in Hollywood, when it came to shooting Boris Karloff in that early talkie *The Mummy* or Abbott and Costello in *Meet the Mummy*, must have been aware of the footage Burton shot of the excavations and of daily life in modern Egypt.

Eight minutes of silent movie abstracted from thirteen hours of documentary reels by Burton along with Albert M. Lythgoe, the head of the Met's Department of Egyptian Art, is the real reason to visit the show. Scenes of labor and dust in the Nile Valley, of exhumations from sealed tombs, of mummy coffins placed in crates that are actually a second funeral, complete with a woodie station wagon for a hearse, make explicit the nature of Egyptian toil. All this in a haze of desert light and billowing dust that lets the decay of the ruins appear present and ongoing.

The moving picture views of daily life in Egypt are of a different order. They show Giza and the Sphinx, of course, but also bustling, random Cairo street scenes chaotic with people and animals and feluccas on the Nile. There is a stretch of travelogue, riding along the Nile on Harkness's private steamer. Watching a 1930s Hollywood movie, we would know exactly who these white-suited men are: They are the professors and plutocrats in pith helmets whose curiosity or ambition or acquisitive nature excite wrath and envy and draw down upon their heads the mummy's curse.

PERFECTION. DESIRE. REGRET. *The Tale of Genji*

Like Homer and Shakespeare, Lady Murasaki occupies a place alone. Epic poetry begins with Homer. Shakespeare invented modern tragedy. Murasaki, a lady-in-waiting in the eleventh-century court of Imperial Japan, wrote the first and still the greatest psychological novel. Her *The Tale of Genji* offers moments straight out of Jane Austen, plots worthy of Henry James, and characters as complex as Marcel Proust's.

The first time I read *The Tale of Genji*, in Arthur Waley's 1920s translation, I felt like William Butler Yeats encountering Byzantium. In Murasaki's tale of tenth-century Heian Imperial Japan, unlimited power and privilege enabled the fortunate to follow the promptings of the heart, for good or ill. With their singing and dancing and painting and poems, the courtiers and women of the palace are akin to the circle surrounding Queen Elizabeth I, but even more refined, and without Francis Walsingham—or the headsman. At least no word of such things reached the women's quarter, from where *The Tale of Genji* is told.

When Edward Seidensticker's version of *Genji* appeared in the mid 1970s, I read the novel a second time, paying more attention to the generation of sons that inhabits the last third of the novel, after Genji's death.

One generation later, Australian Royall Tyler has produced yet another translation, my third encounter with Murasaki's vanished world. This time, it was much easier to keep track of who was who (characters in the Japanese don't have proper names like in English, but are known by rank, or attribute, or family relation, all of which change over the course of a life), and to understand how much time elapsed between chapters. As the characters talk about women and men, or reflect upon the quality of another's calligraphy and skill at music, poetry, and craft, an entire world arises from the page—a world of love, ambition, intrigue, surprise, dashed hope and synesthetic splendor. Murasaki's *Tale of Genji* stands without equal as a nuanced meditation on human perfectability, desire, and regret.

For those unfamiliar with this book—which is longer than all three volumes of *Lord of the Rings*, though shorter than *Remembrance of Things Past*—the first two-thirds of the novel follow the cradle-to-grave career of Genji, the Shining Prince. The story begins with the death of Genji's mother, the emperor's too-beloved minor consort. This early loss determines the trajectory of Genji's career, and frames the entire tale. In this highly wrought world, important emotions are articulated in poetry. The novel's first exchange occurs between the three-year-old Genji's dying mother and the emperor: "'You promised never to leave me, not even at the end,' [the emperor] said, 'and you cannot abandon me now! I will not let you!' She was so touched that she managed to breathe: '*Now the end has come, and I am filled with sorrow that our ways must part: the path I would rather take is the one that leads to life.* If only I had known...'"

In the key of that initial and final uncertainty, Murasaki composes life. "Shining Genji: the name was imposing," the novelist observes at the beginning of her second chapter, "but not so its bearer's many deplorable lapses; and considering how quiet he kept his wanton ways,... whoever broadcast his secrets to all the world was a terrible gossip."

Physically beautiful, wealthy, powerful, cultured, talented, intelligent and good-hearted favorite son though he was, Genji could not be named heir apparent. So the prince served the empire as a commoner. After experiencing one political setback, Genji rose to unrivalled eminence in the Heian Empire: unacknowledged father of one emperor (by the Empress Fujitsubo); father of an empress by his wife from exile, the Akashi Princess; grandfather to the heir apparent; chief minister. A master poet, gifted musician, fascinating dancer, irresistible lover, builder of palaces, connoisseur of the brushstroke, Genji for all his talents is nonetheless an attainable model of what human beings might be—while never denying the truth of what they are.

In many ways, *The Tale of Genji* is a success story like the life of King David. But where David is faithful to the God of Israel, Genji is faithful to his human attachments, to emotional obligations. Where David is the hero of history, Genji is the hero of domesticity. His lapses are rueful rather than sinful. He can have any woman he can see. His difficulties and failures have to do with establishing and sustaining intimacy, attaining not so much carnal union as mutual awareness. The barriers are sometimes erected by his public duties, sometimes by fortune. Whether his affairs succeeded or languished, Genji never forgot a woman—as Murasaki reminds us time and again. This is his perfection.

Western heroism is compounded of the convergence or

dissonance of human impulse and divine law. The story of the Shining Prince oscillates between the frustration and fulfillment of waking desires and glimpses of other powers, other inklings from a world of dreams. The action occurs on the border between the material present and the fullness of time. Here, as in both our sacred and our psychologized world, there are no accidents, only hidden purposes. Here, as elsewhere, the great thing is to know.

The impulses and attachments of Murasaki's characters puzzle those characters as much as they puzzle readers. Musing on his marriage to the daughter of the Akashi prince during a political exile from the capital—an attraction built on the woman's rumored existence and her reputation for musical talent, Genji remarked: "We must have had some connection in a previous life." Just what "connection in a previous life" might entail is revealed in the story of Genji and his young lady (also known as Murasaki). While still in his teens and on one of his first journeys away from the palace, Genji caught sight of a ten-year-old girl through a brushwood fence. "The little girl sat down. She had a very dear face, and the faint arc of her eyebrows, the forehead from which she had childishly swept back her hair, and the hairline itself were extremely pretty. *She* is the one I would like to see when she grows up! Genji thought, fascinated. Indeed, he wept when he realized that it was her close resemblance to the lady who claimed all his heart that made it impossible for him to take his eyes off her."

The child was the niece and image of the Empress Fujitsubo; Fujitsubo was Genji's childhood companion in the palace and first great love. Encouraged to keep each other company by the old emperor—Fujitsubo's husband, Genji's father—the pair once met secretly. The child of that covert connection became the heir apparent. Genji's young lady Murasaki resembled Fujitsubo, yet it was also said that the empress looked very like Genji's mother.

Perhaps that was why the emperor had chosen that young girl to console him after the early death of his beloved favorite. Spiriting Murasaki away from her guardians before her father recalled her existence, Genji established young Murasaki in a wing of his palace. There he personally educated and trained the child to be his life's companion.

The Tale of Genji is a spiritual journey, religious in the personal rather than the institutional sense. What might be mistaken for an extraordinarily overdeveloped æstheticism and emotional pulse-taking are expressions of an impulse to know as much as possible about the knowable—the fashioned and social world. Genji's whole being is engaged in finding a way to navigate the waters of this life through enriching attachments and feelings. Love and loss, beauty and time solemnize every act, every appreciation—a kind of talmudic connoisseurship attentive to the scent, the overtone, the implication of every gesture. Feeling is meaning. And endures.

The characters in *The Tale of Genji* act on impulse and weigh their actions against custom and opportunity. Dreams also exert a force and presence in waking life. This is not some atavistic streak of superstition or of magic. Rather, dreams in this world are a dialogue with or eavesdropped hints from outside the limits of waking vision. Dreams are not to be dismissed as glosses on desire, or as oraculations.

One striking example of the interpenetration of dream and policy is found in a letter the Akashi Prince wrote to his daughter after his granddaughter gave birth to the Heir Apparent (making the old father the future Emperor's great-great-grandfather.) The letter explained how he was able to raise his daughter for a great destiny and sustain his courage all those years in exile from court: "My dear," he wrote, "one night in the second month of the year when you were born, I had a dream. My right hand held up Mount Sumeru, and to the mountain's right and left the sun and moon shed their brightness on the world. I myself stood below, in the shadows under the mountain, and their light did not reach me. I then set the mountain afloat on a vast ocean, boarded a little boat, and rowed away toward the west. That was my dream. I then woke up, and that very morning I, even I, began to hope." The dream tableau was more than a beautiful picture, as the father wrote his daughter, "Then you were conceived. After that, both secular writings and the scriptures gave me so many reasons to believe in dreams that although unworthy I was awed, and I sought to rear you fittingly.... Our young lady has become Mother of the Realm and all that I have prayed for is accomplished. Doubt is no longer possible."

After a valedictory couplet, the old man cautioned: "Do not seek to know the month and day of my death.... Whatever pleasures this life offers, do not forget the life to come. We shall meet again, as long as I reach the place where I long to go."

For a novel written in the eleventh century about a world that even then had vanished, in a translation that has to fold in stylized and alien-to-English poetic forms, *The Tale of Genji* is amazingly fresh and immediate. At least two springs feed the well.

To begin with, *The Tale of Genji* is a performance. Homer and Shakespeare's immediacy flows in part from the doing of voices and acting of parts, whether their tales were told after a banquet, in the marketplace, beside a campfire or at the Globe. For Murasaki, the act of composition is a performance. Large enough to contain the practice of all the other arts, her novel is an improvisation in the same way that the poems her characters produce on occasions are improvised. Not naive, not ignorant, well practiced, yet able to make a stroke like the calligrapher's or watercolorist's brush when the moment arises, Murasaki wrote a book that assumes a reader. *The Tale of Genji* is an extended confidence.

Another source of Murasaki's vitality is the way she tells her story: as a poised, balanced, omniscient participant. Her book is graceful, knowing, ambiguous, horrific, smiling, an immersion in duration. *The Tale of Genji* speaks directly to those who would like not to make a muddle of life, who need to come to terms with mortality, loss, and misapprehension, rather than with glory, triumph, and everlasting fame. The self-consciousness, appreciation for ideas, unerring taste—all this in a form so indissoluble from its content, so beyond fashion, that the chapter where Genji dies is entitled "Vanished into the Clouds," and is blank.

Henry James thought that a story should go on for as long as the thing hangs together and not beyond. *The Tale of Genji* ends some 335 pages and twenty years after the death of its central character. The narrative or karmic thread, which began with the too-passionate and ill-fated love between the emperor and Genji's mother, unspools in the following generation with disappointment of Genji's putative son, Kaoru. This sorry heir of the Shining Prince dispatches the last poem in the book: "*Following the path I trusted would take me to a teacher of the Law,/ I lost my way and wandered a mountain never sought.* Have you forgotten this boy? I keep him beside me in memory of someone who vanished without a trace."

Of course, everyone vanishes without a trace eventually. But some still seem more permanent than others, and some memories are more persistent than most, which slide away like water. That is why stories get told. Murasaki, the most omniscient and honest of narrators, began her story one generation before her hero and concluded it one generation after—stopping at the moment it no longer hangs together.

MUSIC ART

GUM ARABIC: Exiles

Alienation and isolation, yes, but martyrdom and exile are not major themes in English poetry. With the spectacular exceptions of Byron, Shelley, and Ezra Pound, our poets have been perhaps emigres, or tourists, but certainly not Dante at the table of strangers.

Martyrs are even harder to find. There's James Graham, Royalist martyr, who wrote a metrical prayer on the eve of his execution, John Brown, and of course all those Irish ballad heroes in the Roddy McCorley vein. Nameless martyrs and poets without a country are largely a 20th century bequest.

The Palestinian national poet Mahmoud Darwish and the Iraqi socialist Saadi Youssef both write from exile, from inside the Middle East, that land where knowledge of the other goes just so far, and no farther. Darwish is exiled from an exiled nation; Youssef's Iraq is, for all its scars and ruins, one of the oldest places on earth. Both poets have been recently collected in English in books with negative titles. Neither poet is comfortable to encounter.

Unfortunately, It Was Paradise, a selection of poems by Mahmoud Darwish, was translated from the Arabic by a small committee: Munir Akash, the American poet Carolyn Forché, with Sinan Antoon and Amira El-Zein. It contains work from five of Darwish's books published since 1986 (he's published twenty as of 2000), plus three poems written earlier in his career.

I have no sense from the introduction what Darwish's poems are like in Arabic. Judging from the translations, they are classically rhetorical, singing of love and loss (the beloved often the land itself) often in several voices. The longer poems are held together with periodic repeated lines, sometimes varied. Rather than describe the formal aspects of his verse, Carolyn Forché dwells upon the poet's hugely popular espousal of the "poetry of resistance", which she characterizes as an attempt to restore the Palestinian homeland through language. She places him in a poetic class with Federico Garcia Lorca, Pablo Neruda, Osip Mandelstam, Yehuda Amichai and C. P. Cavafy—a range of voices with only the short end of the sociopolitical stick in common.

The lost homeland, the sorrow of exile, the dream of a return, the Fall of Man as experienced in the here-and-now by ethnics and nationals is the stuff of sentimental journalists and and other opportunists whose beat is politics, the organized expression of hatreds. Difficult material from which to fashion a first-hand, that is, first-hand to the reader, rendering of an inhabitable world.

Here's "Neighing on the Slope":

Horses' neighing on the slope. Downward or upward.

I prepare my portrait for my woman to hang on the wall when I die.

She says: *Is there a wall to hang it on?*

I say: *We'll build a room for it. Where? In any house.*

Horses' neighing on the slope. Downward or upward.

Does a woman in her thirties need a homeland to put a picture in a frame?

Can I reach the summit of this rugged mountain? The slope is either an abyss or a place of siege.

Midway it divides. What a journey! Martyrs killing one another.

I prepare my portrait for my woman. When a new horse neighs in you, tear it up.

Horses' neighing on the slope. Upward, or upward.

The woman's question touches me, but the poet's bravura (calling her "my woman", and saying basically hang it on the wall when I die, and keep it there until you find a new lover) puts me off. This may be taken, I guess, as tough-guy talk, or maybe poem noir. The horses and mountain are figurative.

Darwish is in an difficult position. His poems are stocked with gazelles, gypsies, martyrs and prophets, the hoopoe and both testaments, the gods of Egypt and the stars. They lament the lost homeland, the thwarted hope, the consuming rage. But so much impossibility: how can there be a Palestinian nation in language, when there's no Palestinian language, only a long bill of undeniable grievances against history, and those who dispose it? Without the music of the originals, or even the visual rhythm of Arabic script, the translations reveal an awkward abstraction:

"But memory, with two light hands,
hungrily induces fever in the body of the earth.
Memory has the fragrance of a weeping night flower
arousing in the exile's blood a need for singing:
Light up my grief, so I can retrieve my time...."
(from "Mural")

Maybe a poet whose muse is a homeland that exists only in memory, or in prospect, and who pitches his tent in language not in the earth, is also sentenced to at least one remove. And to rhetorical flourish. The opening stanza of the 1976 poem "As Fate Would Have It" *To Rashed Hussein* reads:

> On Fifth Avenue he greeted me and burst into tears.
> He leaned against a wall of glass
> ... New York is without willows.
> He made me cry, and water returned to its rivers.
> We had coffee, and too soon went separate ways.

I appreciate the echoes of Psalm 137 ("By the rivers of Babylon" in the reggae song) where the exiles hang their harps upon the willows. But New York City does have willows, despite the repeated line. The song begins either with a failure of observation, or with a love for its own sound at the expense of descriptive truth. It does, however, assert a willful power.

Saadi Youssef sings a different exilic tune in the third of his three "Solos on the Oud":

> Land where I no longer live,
> distant land
> where the sky weeps,
> where the women weep,
> where people openly read the newspaper.
>
> Country where I no longer live,
> lonely country,
> sand, date palms, and brook.
> O wound and spike of wheat!
> O anguish of long nights!

> Country where I no longer live,
> my outcast country,
> from you I only gained a traveler's sails,
> a banner ripped by daggers
> and fugitive stars,
> *Algiers 16/8/1965*

According to Khaled Mattawa, the translator of *Without an Alphabet, Without a Face*, Saadi Youssef's committed Communism has assured his alienation and exile from every regime in Baghdad since the 1950s. This collection of poems from 1955 to 1997 divides into nine sections, organized by the poet's place of residence. Of those 42 years writing and publishing, perhaps 12 years were spent in Youssef's homeland.

Some of those years were spent in prison. What else can a would-be ruler do with someone who writes (in "Martyrdom" *Basra, 1957*) "The informants rush away,/ tripping on the head of Jesus./ And in the print shops the filthy newspapers/ drink his blood between their coughs,/ black, contemptuous, and prolific." And one year later, pens the little poem "To Socialism"?

Perhaps take pleasure in his work. Even in translation, an honest intelligence shines through.

Early in the last century, when the exile Pound and the émigré T.S. Eliot were inventing modernism and touting World Literature— a thing which has truly come to pass—poets began writing in a way that travelled easily from tongue to tongue. Unrhymed, vernacular, direct, sometimes elliptical and flinty, like Pound's Chinese poems in

English, the international style took root where the League of Nations failed.

While Pound never abandoned the material of his art, the English language, some of his modernist heirs developed an artistic Esperanto, like the French poet Jean Cocteau who avowed that all poetry was written in the same language. Behind his internationalism lay a notion that poetry was, like mathematics or music, a language unto itself, and that the language a poem actually got written in was like the instrument it was scored for. It might be argued from the other side that poetry is wedded to the material it's made in, that the poetry is what gets lost in the translation. Walt Whitman, or Emily Dickinson.

A middle position holds that poetry is a kind of speech, and there are ways that people talk to each other that can be understood from language to language, either because the poetry's at least as well written as prose, or because it speaks from the heart.

The modernist account of the source of poetry resembles the rabbinic fable of the pre-Lapsarian tongue. Briefly told, one day in Eden Adam gave names to every thing, and each name revealed the essence of the thing itself. But Eve fell, Adam fell, language fell into, as John Milton wrote, duality, knowing good and evil or rather, good by evil.

Language fell a second time with the Tower in Babel (that's Uruk, Iraq), which Genesis ascribes to the technological pride of the hunter/city-builder. Babel is of course in Mesopotamia. As are the rivers of Babylon.

Saadi Youssef's 1995 Damascus poem "America, America" has

a kinship with Whitman and Allen Ginsberg, and a sharp eye for the balance of trade. "America," he begins "let's exchange gifts./ Take your smuggled cigarettes/ and give us potatoes." In the spirit of open international exchange, he continues:

> Take James Bond's golden pistol
> and give us vaccines.
> Take your blueprints for model penitentiaries
> and give us village homes.
> Take the books of your missionaries
> and give us paper for poems to defame you.
> Take what you do not have
> and give us what we have.
> Take the stripes of your flag
> and give us the stars.
> Take the Afghan mujahideen beard
> and give us Walt Whitman's beard filled with butterflies.
> Take Saddam Hussein
> and give us Abraham Lincoln
> or give us no one.

Current events is maybe television maybe movies, flashy and two-dimensional and easily personal. History is an echoing hall with indirect light, and is harder to take to heart. In "The Attempt", written in Cairo a year after the America poem, Saadi Youssef fashioned a dialectical materialist's (thesis, antithesis, synthesis) poem in three stanzas that carves in marble the tension between the personal and the historical, between the domestic and the ambitious—the fields of art as well as love and war:

Philip the Macedonian
was the fastest man to answer a question.
He said: "I will remain by the sword.
And I will sleep by the sword—
even if my bones are bleached white—
so long as the sword remains."

But Alexander
did not learn what a son learns
from a father.
He said:
"I will roam the world.
My companions will be
warriors and philosophers
and I will seek answers to
the world's questions."

Alexander
wandered, burning
with the world's questions.
But he remained alone,
without a grave,
and remained distant....
He left only his image:
the face of a boy
who tried to look the world in the face.

One poetry that travels well is the voice of an honest man, talking perhaps to himself.

MUSIC ART

As for the tug-of-war between the prophets of nationality and the one-worlders, the line each side struggles to drag the other across is also drawn by poetry, which marks the place where understanding ends.

TURKISH MODERN: *Snow*

Orhan Pamuk, like Anton Chekhov and Ivan Turgenev, creates characters who are thoroughly human, sympathetic and unique. His people, and he counts himself among them, are both the hostages to personal hope and instruments of historical circumstance; captives of their own convictions and the certainties of others. Like Chekhov, the Turkish storyteller's realism represents the tragic and the comic as the same thing. Like Turgenev, he doesn't allow history or politics to diminish humanity. Neither does he romantically color human weakness or moral lapse. Melodrama is the stuff of distraction. Perfection is the province of monsters and artists.

Pamuk's *Snow* was finished in December, 2001, and published the following year in Istanbul under the title, *Kar*. The principal definition of "kar" is "snow;" so it appears in Maureen Freely's artful translation. Besides snow, the dictionary also defines "kar" as: account; benefit; gain; profit; take; takings; and bank. As a verb, "kar" means: to do, to make, to create; to produce.

The novel is at first glance a sharply drawn picaresque political adventure love story punctuated by odd incident and peculiar violence. Its hero, Ka, is a kind of holy fool for language, a blocked Turkish émigré poet returned from exile in Germany. The plot follows him on journalistic assignment to the provincial city of Kars in Northeast Turkey—adjacent to Georgia, Iran and Syria, once part of Armenia. There's a municipal election coming up, and a series of suicides among schoolgirls forced to abandon their Islamic headscarves has attracted interest in the Western press. Self-consciously a somewhere that's nowhere now, Kars is also the scene of a lot of history, a domicile for religious enthusiasm and long-standing grudge. All the time, it snows.

At second glance, *Snow* reveals itself as an Arabic-Persian-*cum*-self-conscious novel built of a series of tales-within-a-tale. The narrator, Ka's longtime friend who later identifies himself as a novelist named Orhan, announces in the first chapter that the story's told as Ka lived it. The significance of the events for Ka, and so for Orhan, derives initially from the depth and quality of Ka's human encounters as he pursues both love, in the person of the beautiful Ipek, and his assignment for the Istanbul *Republican*.

But it's the return of Ka's poetic inspiration for the term of his stay, the Rilkean angelic speech unbidden and unexpected, that magnetizes Ka's visit to Kars and gives his life narrative meaning. An exaltation may be immeasurable, but that doesn't make it happy.

The poems come to him on the job, or on the way from meeting to meeting. Walking room to room, sometimes in the middle of conversations or interviews with the subjects of his article. No one comes by willing it. They arrive nineteen in all. The connection between the inspirational source and its appearance—between art and life if you will, or truth and speech, or the sacred and profane, eternal and temporal—has a quirky way of sticking an odd elbow through the fabric of being.

One of Ka's journalistic sources is Serdar Bey, the publisher of the *Border City Gazette* (circulation 320). The Gazette practices a kind of pre-emptive journalism: writing stories about future events in the past tense. When Ka reads an article stating that "Ka, the celebrated poet, who is now visiting our city, recited his latest poem, entitled 'Snow'" at a live telecast from the National Theater, he objects: "I don't have a poem called 'Snow,' and I'm not going to the theater this evening."

"Don't be so sure," the publisher replies. "There are those who despise us for writing the news before it happens. They fear us not because we are journalists but because we can predict the future; you should see how amazed they are when things turn out exactly as we've written them. And quite a few things do happen only because we've written them up first. This is what modern journalism is all about...."

Muhtar Bey, Ipek's ex-husband, is the mayoral candidate for the Party of God. He's also an appliance dealer, and a frustrated poet. At his interview, Muhtar describes his secret religious conversion at the lodge of the Kurdish sheikh Saadettin Efendi, his discovery of the spiritual key, and his double life as a secular by day and monotheist by night. Muhtar's conversion led to the end of his marriage (no more sneaking off at night to pray), and to his writing "an important poem. ... As a poem it was flawless. I swear to you," Muhtar told Ka. He sent the flawless poem to a literary magazine, *Achilles Ink*, but it never appeared.

Embittered, Muhtar sought solace from his sheikh. But the old saint, he lamented, "knew nothing of modern poetry, René Char, the broken sentence, Mallarmé, Joubert, the silence of an empty line.

"This undermined my confidence in my sheikh," Muhtar continued. "After all, he hadn't been offering me anything new for some time, just *Keep your heart clean, and God's love will deliver you from oppression* and eight or ten other lines like that."

Ipek, when queried about the suicides, had said, "The men give themselves to religion, and the women kill themselves."

Blue, a celebrity political Islamist hiding in Kars, who came to Kars to stop the suicide epidemic, suddenly pulls his interviewer, Ka, close to him, kisses him on both cheeks and says: "You are a modern-day dervish. You've withdrawn from the world to devote yourself to poetry. You would never be the pawn of those who would denigrate innocent Muslims."

At the beginning of his story, while the bus to Kars pushed on through the blizzard, Pamuk quoted a line from one of Ka's early poems: "It snows only once in our dreams." This only-onceness would be a trope on the scientist's rule that every snowflake has six sides and crystalline structure, and every snowflake is unique. It's a simple leap from snowflake, to individual soul, though the snowflake melts and soul does not; the snowflake-to-poem correlation would be in the unique utterance inside the recognized shape. The difference, of course, is that the poem does not melt like the snowflake, and unlike the soul, is material, is recorded.

The Novelist Orhan, sifting through the notebooks and effects Ka left in the four years following his journey to Kars, is able to reconstruct in vivid detail the circumstances and perhaps even the stimuli of Ka's inspirations, 19 in all, in a fashion that's to me entirely convincing. Orhan describes his novelistic sources, his retracing Ka's steps and talking to all the surviving participants in those sublime days. Orhan discovers a map drawn in one of Ka's many notebooks of exegesis that he filled while refining and arranging his book of poems, *Snow*. The map is a snowflake: three intersecting axes, with three poems each at six ends, and one poem in the middle.

It's possible, reading from the list of Ka's poems in the order he wrote them at the back of the book, to pinpoint the page in the novel where each poem occurred. Only the poems themselves, set down in the poet's green notebook, are missing.

Prose isn't a happy environment for poetry, anyway. For every successful literary biography like, say, *Shelley: The Pursuit*, there are hundreds of labored exegeses and self-serving interpreters; Murasaki's poems in the *Tale of Genji* are social occasions, not motives; the *Vita Nuova* succeeds as a Tale of Poetry, but Orhan Pamuk is not trying to convince us that Ka is Dante. Subjected to the winds of taste, the poems in "Snow" would melt.

The absent poems are the novelist's pretext, not the poet's. These poems, like the region where they come from and, like the white space in Mallarmé, draw strength and reality from their absence. All implication, with no information to disturb the void.

The novel has a sociability and what I might call a kind of practical humor that puts one foot firmly on the journalistic earth. On the other hand, this book's intimations of meaning and respect for the human heart point toward the empty shelf with the dust outline where the Grecian Urn once stood. Snow can be read like a dream or dream foretold.

Take the single syllable, Ka. The modernist says: "K"–that's Kafka's Joseph K. Even more, *Snow*'s thwarted guilt and oppression suggest *The Trial* and *The Castle*. Ka's goofy, inept and self-defeating tango with the possible marks him as an islamic soulmate of Kafka in his *Letters to Milena*, advancing toward and recoiling from the prospect of human happiness. There's hope, the sage of Prague observed, but not for us.

KA, as his name appears in a typo in the *Border City News*, are also the initials of Kemal Ataturk, founder and modernizer of the Turkish secular republic. A British Imperial legacy like Turkey's national borders, "Ka" is also the python (a python's a Greek prophet) from Kipling's *Jungle Books*.

Closer to home, and older and deeper, "ka" is that part of the Egyptian soul where the individual personality resides, and survives death.

In Chapter Thirty-one: THE SECRET MEETING AT THE HOTEL ASIA, competing factions in Kars convene to write a statement which Ka is supposed to get published in Germany. Only appearance in the Western press will make the people of Kars real, not for the West, perhaps not even for Istanbul, but most certainly for themselves. One high school student wants the statement to read: "We're not stupid, we're just poor." It's the cry of the overlooked, the voice of one who, could he only prove he exists, might survive life.

One difference between political life and the arts is that a successful politics cannot leave everybody on the other side dead. It has to seek accommodation. That each side hates all others is no wonder. But to be social means one's willing to live and let live, to live in suspense. Only plays and novels and movies have to end in resolution. Preferably in a return to the harmony of the beginning, which is also an invention.

In an essay, "The Anger of the Damned," which appeared in the November 1, 2001 issue of the *New York Review of Books,* Orhan Pamuk wrote about his desperate solitude as he sat in an Istanbul coffee house and watched the World Trade Center towers collapse. Pamuk had lived in New York, walked the downtown streets, met with people in the towers. Walking out of the coffee house, Pamuk met an old man, a neighbor who had not yet seen the horror on TV. "Sir," his neighbor said, "... they have bombed America. They did the right thing."

Pamuk was three months short of completing *Snow* when this voice of higher resentment led him to wonder if the American response would include a righteous nationalistic rage where "some will find it easy to speak words that might lead to the slaughter of other innocent people. In view of this," Pamuk allowed, "one wants to say something."

He already had. The novel *Snow* now reads like a kind of pre-emptive prophecy. It's filled with the voices of those beyond the reach of glamor, magic or æstheticism, voices that cluster around a novelist's sublime poet and his imaginary poems. The novelist also lays the only onstage murders at the feet of the two men in Kars "who have read T.S. Eliot." Remember the composer Karlheinz Stockhausen's unfortunate favorable "review" which admired the orchestration of the WTC attacks? The idea's to be only *half* in love with easeful death.

MUSIC ART

THE ORIGINAL TRUE HISTORY: *Don Quixote*

What kind of proprietary relationship exists between the writer and his character? Hamlet, Falstaff, Lear and company are always Shakespeare's. They are giants of the stage, along with their mysterious creator. Deeply as they speak to the human heart, they don't leave the boards, walk out through the audience, and exit to the street. What writer could name a character "Hamlet" and think even for a moment that it would not conjure Shakespeare's?

Doctor Johnson, an historical personage, may live by dint of James Boswell's journalising, but the author of *The Dictionary* had a larger-than-life existence of his own. Thanks to the heap of minute particulars amassed by Boswell, there is little chance of anyone "being" or invoking "another" Samuel Johnson. The obverse of a character imagined so vividly that he seems real, like the mural painted by Apelles that birds tried to light on, Boswell's subject is an actuality meticuluously documented by an imagination in love with another man's life.

Don Quixote presents itself as a personal history, framed in the conventions of a courtly romance. Miguel de Cervantes, the author of record, was perhaps descended from Spanish Jews on his mother's side. As a young man, he fought with the Spanish navy alongside the vessels of Venice and the Papal States in the Battle of Lepanto and was wounded in that victory over the Ottoman fleet. Sailing home four years later, Cervantes was captured by Barbary pirates, and endured five years of slavery in Algiers before his family finally ransomed him. Back in Spain and dirt-poor, he worked for a time as a collector of taxes beginning around the defeat of the Spanish Armada, only to be imprisoned for peculation, or incompetence, or some other haplessness. One tradition holds that Cervantes began writing his *Ingenious Gentleman: Don Quixote of La Mancha* while still in prison, in 1598. Part One of the novel was published in 1605. It was an instant success, for its publisher if not for the author.

Part Two of *Don Quixote* appeared in 1615, about one year before Cervantes' death on April 23, 1616. As the *Second Part of The Ingenious Gentleman... by Miguel de Cervantes Saavedra, Author of the First Part* makes abundantly clear, Cervantes was galvanized by the popularity of a false sequel. *The Second Part of the Exploits of Don Quixote of La Mancha,* by Fernandez de Avellaneda, made a mock of his character. So again Cervantes picked up his pen, to defend the honor and dignity of the Knight of the Sad Countenance (called the Sorrowful Face, in Edith Grossman's spirited, lucid and wholly pleasurable translation), and the integrity of his imagination.

The true adventures of the real Don Quixote are only found in Cervantes' novel. But his knight has ridden clear off the page and into the minds of all, whether they've read his adventures or no. The novel has fostered such inventions as an English song cycle by William Purcell, a 19th-century Russian ballet, an 18th-century French ditto, and a German romantic ballet set by Felix Mendelssohn. Also numbered among its progeny are a 17th-century French stage comedy, operas by Jules Massenet and Georg Philip Telemann. Tobias Smollett did a complete English translation, Mikhail Bulgakov made the Don into Russian. There are a Hebrew

Don Quixote, the Broadway musical *Man of La Mancha* and, most recently a film, *Lost in La Mancha*.

Translations aside, none of these *hommages* and spin-offs of *Don Quixote* has a life independent of the novel. Perhaps truest to the quixotic spirit is *Lost in La Mancha,* which documents celluloid medievalist and former Monty Python trouper Terry Gilliam's failed attempt to film his favorite novel. Watching, it's hard to tell where inspiration edges into madness, where history leaves off and embroidery takes over, what action is scripted and when real misfortune begins. The documentary stars Gilliam as himself, the script writer and director; the actor who is unable to play Don Quixote for medical reasons is Jean Rochefort; Johnny Depp plays Johnny Depp signed to play Sancho Panza. One Fred Millstein plays himself in the role of "production guarantor." Jeff Bridges narrates. Orson Welles appears courtesy of the archives. The rains, the banks, and conflicting schedules conspire to curse Gilliam's production as absolutely as any evil enchanter could. Not even the windmill scene is completed. The documentary ends with a plea for a new backer to finance *Don Quixote*.

What is the original of the true history of Don Quixote?

Part one, the first eight chapters, sets the Don upon the path of chivalry, and returns him dubbed and drubbed to his home village. This opening sally parodies those popular romances in Don Quixote's library, which the priest and the barber consider each by each, and consign to the flames. After the *auto-da-fe*, the tale cuts free of received folly. Don Quixote's second venture into the Spanish countryside, this time accompanied by his squire and conversational complement Sancho Panza, is one as yet untold.

Cervantes refers to himself as "the second author" of his book. He claims that he suspended chapter eight in mid-gesture because he could not discover what came next. Yet this second author refused "to believe that so curious a history would be subjected to the laws of oblivion,... and so,... he did not despair of finding the conclusion to this gentle history...." One day in the market of Toledo, Cervantes happened upon a boy selling a bundle of old books and papers. Answering his curiosity, Cervantes plucked a volume from the pile. It was written in Arabic. No problem. The Spaniard easily found a Morisco who spoke both Castilian and Arabic (indeed, it would have been even easier to find a Hebrew-speaking Christian there, had one been called-for.) Cervantes handed the volume to the Moor, and asked him to interpret. The Morisco opened the book, and began to laugh. So was discovered the *History of Don Quixote of La Mancha. Written by Cide Hamete Benengeli, an Arab Historian.*

To claim that a book is actually the translation of an older manuscript from another language was a common device in volumes of chivalry, and others, as our translator explains in one of her illuminating footnotes. But I take this nudge from Cervantes as something more than conventional. *Don Quixote* is the work of an old, wounded soldier, not a literary *pastiche*. The writer had lived and fought among Arabs; Spain had a long and glorious Moorish history only officially expunged in 1492. And the first real chivalric romance, as distinct from the ruck of 16th-century pulp taken from the Quixote's personal library and fed to the flames, was written in Arabic.

Antar: A Bedoueen Romance, as translated by Terrick Hamilton in 1819, would fill over 4000 pages were the entire original ever to make it into English. It celebrates the exploits of an historical figure, Antara Ibn Shaddad, from the time known as the Ignorance, before the calling of Mohammed. Warrior, lover, author of one of the "Seven Odes" written on banners in gold ink and hung in the Ka'aba in Mecca, Antar was the black son of a sheik of the tribe of Abs by an Ethiopian concubine. His *Romance*, attributed to Al-Asmai, renowned Basran scholar at the court of Harun ar-Rashid, was as popular in the Arab-speaking world as the *1001 Nights*. Dating from the time of Charlemagne, the work was composed before the *Poem of the Cid* and the *Song of Roland*, not to mention all those epics celebrating the Jerusalem Crusades.

The French artists Robert and Sonia DeLaunay practiced what they called "simultaneity." Their æsthetic theory stated that no color exists alone, but only appears when in the company of at least one other color. There is no such thing as "red." There is only red next to blue, or green, or yellow or black. And red next to blue differs from the same pigment beside yellow. Don Quixote, the knight errant, starts out as a reader, but only lives as an actor and speaker. His actions alone, before he rides with Sancho, are slapstick cruel, and even grotesque. Paired with the earthy Sancho, his discourses become part of an ongoing conversation. And his chivalric imaginings reshape the landscape, just as Jacob dreaming in a empty place with a rock for a pillow could awake and see that empty place was none other but the house of God, the gateway to heaven.

For Cervantes, that most serious reader, it was not enough to open discourse via Don Quixote with the world as it might be, and with Sancho as it hath ever been. Through his Arab historian, and the secret Jews in the Toledo market, he also enters into a conversation with what once really was, and how it still is behind the screen of orthodoxy. By constantly poking at the edges of his own conventions, Cervantes manages to have it both ways, to make a fiction that insists upon the existence of a higher fact.

The narrative deadpan self-consciousness liberates Don Quixote from the constraints of literature, of unreality, of the Inquisition. The Knight of the Sorrowful Face might even have escaped from the confines of his own life story, except that the author(s) return Quixote to his senses. The return to what may be sanity, or maybe a transfiguration, ends with a novelistic death so unwelcome to this reader that it makes a real grief.

The hero began his story as a 50-year-old gentleman named Quixada, or Quexada, or Quexana. Bedeviled by his reading and perhaps an intimation that the life he'd lived was not one he believed in, or perhaps because he was no longer of an age to love a woman, all that remained for him was to declare his love for an idea. Whatever the impulse, he entered the lists as Don Quixote of La Mancha.

Defeated at last in combat by another knight, the disguised bachelor Sanson Carrasco, the melancholy knight undergoes one final transformation. To the assembled friends called to his bedside to hear his will, he will tell no more tales. Instead, he declares that "Those [tales] that until now...have been real, to my detriment, will, with the help of heaven, be turned to my benefit by my death." And more: "Let us go slowly, for there are no birds today in yesterday's nests. I was mad, and now I am sane; I was Don Quixote of La Mancha, and now I am, as I have said, Alonso Quixano the Good." Then Don Quixote collapsed on his bed and, three days later, he died.

The scribe (no name given) drew up one more document, attesting to the natural death of Don Quixote, so that no author other than Cide Hamete Benengeli himself would falsely resurrect him.

Cide Hamete, who may or may not be Miguel de Cervantes but is surely not the contemptible Avellaneda, then spoke a valediction to his pen that equals Prospero's adjuration of his books. Cautioning "presumptuous and unscrupulous historians" against profaning his enterprise, the Arab declares:

"For me alone was Don Quixote born, and I for him; he knew how to act, and I to write...." Then someone very like the second author takes one last swing at that false history which, had the inspired Cervantes not taken arms against it, would surely be lost in oblivion.

THE SERVICE: Poems for Yom Kippur

The art historian Meyer Schapiro once told a young poet that the greatest thing about poetry was that it was "written for God." The joke is not just about the marketplace, it's also about the audience, about who cares and who pays attention.

Even the great masters of English religious poetry, William Blake and John Milton, command less attention than a rerun rock concert. Except for verse dramas, poetry is read and experienced one-on-one, and has no authentic social occasion or unembarrassed public moment.

Piyyut, Jewish liturgical poetry, is different. *Avodah*, poems written for the Yom Kippur service, are first of all versified renditions of the talmudic *Mishnah Yoma*. They assume an audience of more or less learned Jews gathered on the tenth day of Tishrei to participate in the ritual that atones for all the sins of Israel, personal and public.

That rite, performed against the backdrop of historic loss and a hope for redemption, very well may be as effective as the Levitical scapegoat bearing the collective guilt released to wander the wilderness. Only the Day itself corresponds to the requirements of Torah. How can the Temple sacrifice be performed when there is no Temple? The modern state of Israel is not the Two Kingdoms united under David and divided after Solomon; and its Jerusalem is not a happy home.

Prophecy ceased in Israel with the fall of the First Temple. Rabbinic Sages, the heroes of the Talmud, through ongoing discussion and disputation rather than inspiration became the illuminators of the word darkened by time. Their legends and methods brought forward the meaning of Torah in the language and experience of the present.

During the Bar Kokhba rebellion in the years following the Roman destruction of the Second Temple, an entire generation of Sages was martyred. Rabbi Akiva, an equal of Moses in the tradition, was flayed alive as he recited the *Shema* ("Hear, O Israel, the Lord our God is one").

Their banishment from Jerusalem set the Jews adrift, but the next generation realized that their oral tradition, like the Torah at the close of the Babylonian Captivity, needed to be written down, or be lost. The Talmuds of Babylon and Palestine, in company with the Masoretic edition of the Jewish Bible, transformed a local cult and dispossessed nation into the People of the Book.

Avodah, dating from about the fourth century, are the poets' response to a practical problem: how can we celebrate rites specific to a place that is no more?

The eight poems in *Avodah: Ancient Poems for Yom Kippur*, translated for the first time into English, propound a substitute Temple in poetic space. If Israel will gather in time, the Divine Presence may be called down to an altar in the hearts of the people. Israel join to the Torah in the same way that its sins may be borne by the scapegoat, even though there is no more Temple, nor wilderness at hand, nor even an actual sacrifice. It's both a social memory, and a communal sublimation.

The editors/translators of this book, Michael D. Swartz and Joseph Yahalom, do an intelligent and nuanced job introducing the poems, summarizing the scriptural, historical, linguistic, artistic and hermeneutic traditions that resonate in the Hebrew originals. The sacred poetry is dense and allusive.

What sings in the originals with their sources in the Prophets and Psalms can only inform the English. Reading these accounts, broken into verse lines but otherwise prosy, is like encountering Milton or Blake minus the music. In all cases, the more information you have about the text, the more you get.

The Yom Kippur poems begin with an invocation to the Creator, rehearse the history of Israel from the Creation forward, then turn to the preparation of the High Priest, the performance of the sacrifices and the successful conclusion of the rite of Atonement.

Much of the poets' art involved finding new yet communicative ways to name and invoke Biblical and natural matters. For example, "Those aware of good and evil" is a trope for Adam and Eve. Cain is called "The child of thieves." "That which He holds in the hollow of His hand," is water. The technique, called *kinnui* in Hebrew, resembles Icelandic bardic kennings like "mother of ice" for water.

There is an unvoiced melody in the Talmudic literature that flows from the evenness of its temper, the gravity of disputation, and its resistance to any final disposition. It's found in the suggestion that when painting a wall, some part must be left uncovered, as a token that the Creation is not yet finished.

The divergent approaches to familiar figures in these poems endow the old stories with the power of new prospects. The seminal, epical and anonymous *Az Be-'En Kol* ("When All Was Not") portrays the boor (Adam) and the arouser (Eve) as rude and ignorant, rather than as the flawed perfections of the *Zohar* or, more familiarly, 'Paradise Lost':

> They did not sleep
> one night in honor,
> for the one who is like a beast
> did not understand honor.
>
> They were expelled from Eden
> to devour food in sweat,
> for pleasure
> is not fitting for a fool.

Another unattributed poem, *Atah Konanta 'Olam Me-Rosh* ("You Established the World from the Beginning") approaches the same material from the other side of the Divine, the side of mercy:

> You formed from the earth
> a lump of soil in Your image
> and commanded him
> concerning the tree of life.
>
> He forsook Your word
> and he was forsaken from Eden
> But You did not destroy him
> for the sake of the work of Your hands.

Three of the poems in this volume were written by Yose ben Yose, a fifth-century *payetan* (poet). *Azkir Gevurot Elohah* ("Let Me Recount the Wonders of God") prods the memory of the congregation:

> When the Lord conceived,
> when God invented,
> He consulted but none could prevent Him,
> He spoke and none constrained Him.
>
> He speaks and fulfills,
> decrees and enacts,
> He is strong enough to support it [the world]
> heroic enough to bear it.

Atah Konanta 'Olam be-Rov Hesed ("You Established the World in Great Mercy"), another complete *Avodah* by Yose ben Yose, speaks directly to God on behalf of Israel. It reminds the Creator that the world "will not shatter/...and will not collapse/ from the weight of transgression and sin." The poem then points to the Torah, and recalls that

> While the earth was still
> desert and wasteland,
> You amused Yourself with the glow of the Law,
> and it frolicked at Your feet.

The sublime in literature, rare in English poetry outside Blake and Milton (though Shelley hits it in "Ozymandias") abounds in these ancient Jewish poems. And not only in paraphrases of the Creation, or as in a Psalm where the mountains skip like rams. A long passage in the *Az Be-'En Kol* describes the vestments of the High Priest, the heir of Aaron. Every stone on the breastplate is expounded as a tribe of Israel. After donning the breastplate, the priest who is to conduct the sacrifices of atonement...

> ... put on the sash,
> like a belt on his loins,
> to cleave the place of fire
> to the Fire Consuming Fire.
>
> He wore it on top of it,
> Like a dressing for a wound
> to wear over a ruin
> as vast as the sea.
>
> It was hollow
> and made of embroidered work
> to revive our hollow corpses
> and to stop our slaying.
>
> He girded himself
> and concealed its end inside,
> like the rivers that go around,
> ending at the sea.

"The place of fire" is a metonym for Israel; the "Fire Consuming Fire" is God; the "ruin vast as the sea" is Jerusalem. I can't think of another poem in any language which does so much with a belt on a robe.

MUSIC ART

CONCEALED, REVEALED: *The Zohar*

Sefer ha-Zohar—variously known as *The Zohar*, *The Book of Radiance*, or the *Book of Splendor*—is the central text of Jewish Kabbalah. Written by Moses de Leon (1250–1305), a Castilian Jew and member of a circle of Spanish kabbalists, the manuscript appeared and circulated piecemeal over the last two decades of the thirteenth century. When Ferdinand and Isabella expelled all unconverted Jews from their reconquered Spain in 1492, the kabbalists carried the *Zohar* with them to refuges in North Africa, Turkey, Babylon, and Palestine.

The *Zohar* is an enigmatic text. Moses de Leon wrote his book in a literary Aramaic that was never spoken in any part of Arabic or Roman Spain, and he mixed it with biblical Hebrew. In form, the text is a commentary on the Five Books of Moses, but the commentary is not intended to lay bare the meaning of the text, as does, say, the French medieval rabbinic commentary by Rashi. Rather, it records an oral tradition that conveyed the inner meanings (the "Divine Chariot") of the Torah taught by Moses to the elders in the wilderness and transmitted through Joshua and the judges to the prophets, and down to the sages of the great assembly.

The last generation of the sages was martyred by the Romans in the middle of the second century in the suppression of the Bar Kokhba rebellion. Faced with the prospective annihilation of the oral tradition, Rabbi Yehuda ha-Nasi compiled and edited the Talmud, so the evolved wisdom of Israel would be preserved. All is not settled in the Talmud, which teaches method as well as matter, and its unfinished business provides topics and models for discussion to this day.

Nor did all the sages of the great assembly perish like Rabbi Akiba. Rabbi Simeon ben Yohai and his son Rabbi Elazar concealed themselves for ten years in a cave. After they emerged, a circle of companions dedicated to discussion of the Torah formed around them. The *Zohar* is Moses de Leon's record of their commentary, or midrash.

By the middle of the thirteenth century, this other oral tradition was in danger. The teaching handed down from Rabbi Simeon and his company of scholars to the kabbalists of Castile, Andalusia, and Catalonia (along with a library of mystical texts that are known only because the *Zohar* alludes to them) was now caught between the struggles of Latin Catholicism and Arabic Islam.

One century before, Moses Maimonides wrote his introduction to the Talmud in Arabic, the language of philosophy and governance, for the cultured populations of all faiths. The earlier Hebrew poets of Moorish Spain also composed their prose works in Arabic, like Jehudah Halevi's defense of Judaism, *al-Kuzari*, or the philosophical treatises of Solomon ibn Gabirol.

Moses de Leon, however, wrote his book in a literary Aramaic unknown to southern Spain. The artificial literary dialect conceals its meaning in plain sight: To read the original is to be confounded. Even to be introduced, the *Zohar* must be coaxed out of its linguistic cave by translators and expounders.

Such translators and expounders have a long history. Sefad, a village located on the Sea of Galilee, was home in the sixteenth century to a circle of influential kabbalists. Chief among them was Rabbi Isaac Luria, though he only taught there for two years before his early death at thirty-eight. Luria was the first man in nearly three centuries inspired and confident enough to extract the kernel from the *Zohar*'s Aramaic husk.

Luria left no writings, only disciples. As transmitted by his chief disciple Hayyim Vital, Lurianic Kabbalah found in the *Zohar*, among other things, a key to unlock the coming of Moshiach and the Jews' deliverance. Luria's teachings guided Nathan of Gaza, a scholar of the mid-seventeenth century, eminent as a healer of sick souls. When the disturbed Rabbi Sabbatai Ṣevi approached Rabbi Nathan for relief from his messianic delusions, Nathan instead played Elijah and proclaimed Ṣevi the messiah. The kabbalist justified every strange act of his messiah's career, up to and including Ṣevi's conversion to Islam.

The significant portion of eastern European Jewry that embraced this messiah over orthodox rabbinic opposition could not, however, follow him into apostasy. From the embers of their profound disappointment, Hasidic Judaism was born. The pious retained the habits of the kabbalistic circle directed by an inspired teacher, with the *Zohar* as a central text.

Only in the past fifty years or so have the peculiar gifts of the Hasidic communities and their stories of the Baal Shem-Tov been appreciated in the West. Nineteenth-century enlightened Jewry, as exemplified by Heinrich Graetz's six-volume standard *History of the Jews*, dismissed Kabbalah as *shtetl* superstition inimical to modern thought, unacceptable even to the philosophical Talmudism derived from Maimonides. In other words, Kabbalah was an embarrassment to those who would assimilate, who would live in the present and in the world.

But in the early 1920s, the German scholar Gershom Scholem immigrated to Palestine, where he pursued his study of Jewish mysticism until his death in 1989. Facing down the received condescension of reasonable Judaism, Scholem wrote a number of volumes that restored intellectual respectability to Jewish mystical literature. Scholem's *Sabbatai Ṣevi: The Mystical Messiah*, published in Hebrew in 1957 and in English in the early 1970s, placed the *Zohar*, Lurianic Kabbalah, and messianic longing in historical and intellectual context. Scholem's pioneering scholarship was also the departure point for a new generation of kabbalists, speculative and practical. Some, like Moshe Idel, have explored the origins and experience of Jewish mysticism. Others have parsed and translated the text.

Sefer ha-Zohar knocked around in manuscript for two centuries before it first was published in book form, in Italy, around 1559. The Torah commentary ran to three volumes; other, fragmentary commentaries were collected in two separate editions. Because Moses de Leon's work emerged episodically, and the author never had an opportunity to redact his own manuscript, the order of presentation has been a subject of dispute.

The first translation of the *Zohar* into English, by Harry Sperling and Maurice Simon, was published by the Soncino Press in 1934. The translators' professed desire to render the *Zohar* intelligible led them to omit passages and to organize the apparent jumble typographically and paragraphically. Their prose, they wrote, attempts a faithful account of every word in some of those "highly enigmatical" parts where "in the absence of an authentic tradition their true meaning is a matter of conjecture." It reads like the work of well-educated Englishmen, wishing not to sound over-abrupt.

Another edition available to the English reader is the 1989 translation of Isaiah Tishby's three-volume *The Wisdom of the Zohar: An Anthology of Texts*. Tishby first translated the *Zohar* into Hebrew, then arranged the midrash thematically rather than in scriptural order. Tishby comments extensively on the Zoharic passages. His book clarifies in a way that the Soncino *Zohar* does not. It is Jerusalem-centered, rather than London-based. But for all its welcome illumination, Tishby's *Zohar* comes to us at the third remove: from Aramaic through Hebrew into English.

Tishby is not alone. Of the twenty-six (by my count) translations of the *Zohar* into modern languages, seven are into Hebrew. There are two German translations, one French; the rest are in English; all are twentieth century. Michael Berg's twenty-three-volume translation is an English version of Rabbi Yehudah Ashlag's mid-twentieth-century Hebrew translation and commentary. The sole "older" translation of the *Zohar* is the 1684 *Kabbala Denudata*, in Latin. So modern Jews (like their medieval European counterparts, wishing to acquaint themselves with Maimonides' *The Guide of the Perplexed*) have had to wait for the *Zohar* to be translated into Hebrew.

Unlike most books, the *Zohar* treats language like a thing, a material condensation or emanation of the Divine. For Moses de

Leon, the spoken word was the creative instrument. Letters of the Hebrew alphabet themselves possess numerical and visual-formal properties. Their numerical and pictorial relations constitute an atomic or genetic structure, an invisible dimension active in the making of this world—and the other world, as well.

Daniel Matt's landmark translation of the *Zohar* from the original tongues into English opens with a diagram of the Ten *Sefirot*: the schema that represents the crowns or emanations of the Divine, the attributes and body parts, the male and female of both this world and the world to come. Every work about the *Zohar* begins with a discussion of this figure, which is an over-determined and vastly more complex predecessor of the European Renaissance's white-magical astrological Vitruvian man. It summarizes the universe in a glyph.

Supplementing this emblematic and bewildering diagram of kabbalist wisdom, Matt offers the bedrock acoustic of speech itself. His writing insists on its status as living language, even as it hides behind the appeal to tradition or its profession as a translation. He has invented an English *Zohar* that sounds like literary Aramaic in the same way that Ezra Pound invented an English poetry that sounds like Chinese. Both midrash and poetry are ancient novelties.

Sometimes it's hard to tell midrash from a poem. For example: "Rabbi El'azar said, 'When the blessed Holy One created the world, it was on condition: "When Israel appears, if they accept the Torah, fine; if not, I will reduce you back to chaos." The world was not firmly established until Israel stood at Mount Sinai and accepted Torah; then the world stood firm. Ever since that day, the blessed Holy One has been creating worlds. What are they? Human couplings, for since then the blessed Holy One has been matchmaking, proclaiming: "The daughter of so-and-so for so-and-so!" These are the worlds He creates.'" This English literary Aramaic uses concrete language and figures of speech that will strike the ear as odd—but that's because odd is what's going on. Despite the advanced condition of its learning, the voice retains its tribal accent.

In place of assumptions about the talmudical, mathematical and hermeneutic sophistication of readers, Matt offers an exhaustive commentary and apparatus in his footnotes. The dialogue between the text and notes generates the real music of this work. Sometimes the notes expand the gnomic text; sometimes the notes connect the narrative and descriptive events of the text with the schematic cosmological plan, or the hermeneutics of interpretation. Sometimes a story told in the text is answered with another story in the footnotes.

Typographically, the text of this English *Zohar* rides above the translator's commentary, like the upper world above the lower, or the world we live in, and the world to come. Every time a fundamental principle is invoked in the text, the note cites the principle explicitly, and points forward and backward to other appearances. So certain notes recur, such as "If one comes to defile himself, he is provided an opening; if one comes to purify himself, he is assisted." Or "The world on high needs the arousal of the world below."

It is not easy to argue or to swallow that the life one has is the life one chooses. Understanding how the world-to-come is always present, and that the creative source which the quick intuit, depends upon and responds to us, is a still harder stretch. Reading the *Zohar* affords even a non-observant, speculative Jew like myself the opportunity to participate in an act of divine imagination. Moses de Leon does more than tell stories through old Rabbis, though the stories do smile, and Torah glints like a gem in a sunny streambed. His writing is a ladder between the here and the hereafter, longing and fulfillment, the head and the heart.

CHINESENESS: *The Late Tang*

Until the sea change of the Tang, Chinese poetry was measured by and read in light of the Confucian *Book of Songs*. The "Great Preface," which every aspirant to Imperial service would have had by heart, states that "the sounds of an age of order are peaceful and happy—its government is in harmony." By contrast, "the sounds of a world in disorder are bitter and full of rancor—its government is perverse." Therefore, as a practical matter, "to understand how things have succeeded and how they have failed, to move Heaven and Earth, and to stir supernatural beings, there is nothing more appropriate than poetry."

Stephen Owen has written four monumental literary studies: *The Making of Early Chinese Classical Poetry*; *The Poetry of the Early Tang*; *The Great Age of Chinese Poetry: The High Tang*; and *The Late Tang: Chinese Poetry of the Mid-Ninth Century (827-860)*. There, he details for English speakers that moment in Chinese history when the 1000-year-old way of writing and thinking about poetry changed. Owen's other major work, the just-shy-of-2000-page annotated thematic-generic-historic *An Anthology of Chinese Literature: Beginnings to 1911*, makes a kind of epic, in translation, of the entire Chinese poetic canon.

These books are not prose settings for Chinese poems in English that speak for themselves, the way Ezra Pound's "translation" of Rihaku's "The River Merchant's Wife: A Letter" stands on it own. Instead, they are prose explorations of poetics, of the ways poetry is made, and read, in a far off time and place.

Nonetheless, Owen's scholarship resonates. When he talks about the difference between contemporary reputation and canonic stature, about the tendency of poetry to either tie itself too closely to the immediate, or to cut itself off from extra-literary concerns, to aim high or pitch low, he could as easily be talking about present-day tension between rhetoric and common sense, between technique and truth, tradition and inspiration, between art and earnest.

The Late Tang closely considers the styles, genres and literary schools that developed as the Great Age of Chinese Poetry ripened into the matured, self-conscious art of the middle 9th century. Five poets—Li He, Du Mu, Cao Tang, Li Shangyin and Wen Tingyun—dominate Owen's account, with Li Shangyin receiving the dragon's share of ink. In poems and prose, these poets reflected upon their inherited tradition, and upon each other.

The Annals of the Grand Historian of China writes history two ways. In one, narratives recount the fates of nations and dynasties through the words and actions of individuals, like Herodotus, Thucydides and Tacitus combined. A Plutarchan second cycle consists of famous lives, sometimes of large figures in the narrative, sometimes of minor players in affairs, but important in other ways. Famous is not the same as good. Also, the Grand Historian, Ssu-ma Ch'ien, makes a chapter of his own unfortunate career.

Owen notes that part of how a poem is read depends on whose name is attached to it, and that the Grand Historian's was the first authorial voice in post-Classical China. As Chinese poetry evolved away from the anonymous *Book of Songs*, and came to describe more and more the world of the poet, a poet's biography became more than part of his material. The life story also colored how a poem was read. This prose setting, for individual poems as well for lives, offers access to the living part of the poetry in translation, whether or not one can hear an actual voice. For readers with no Chinese, like myself, the stories are the equivalent of oral tradition.

This may be why, as spirited English, prose Chinese succeeds where verse for the most part doesn't. Ezra Pound probably wrote such beautiful "Chinese" poems because he was convinced that the ideographs were pictures of things, which he could interpret by looking. Yet his "Canto XIII" (Kung walked/ by the dynastic temple/ and into the cedar grove...) which collages Confucian Classics dialogue with scenes from an Idaho boyhood is very close to measured prose, like passages in Wordsworth's "Immortality Ode." Canto XIII's balanced language suggests that there once lived people who knew more and were better than we are (a Chinese of the imagination). Standing tradition on its head, Pound's English implies a literature, a history, an ethic of other possibilities, out there in the white spaces beyond the margins.

By the Late Tang, poets were writing about themselves and their predecessors. A contemporary's view of any poet may be at odds with the poet's self-image, the æsthetic of either a detractor or an admirer, as well as the poet's place accorded in the canon.

Take the story of Li He's literary remains. He died 816, at 26, without offspring. The poet's literary executor, Shen Shushi, kept Li's collected poems, but forgot about it, trundling them about with his baggage for 15 years. One night while staying at his brother's place, drunk and restless, Shen came upon Li's manuscript. Stung by guilt, he sent a midnight message to a young writer in his brother's service, and asked him to write a preface. The writer, Du Mu, at first refused. Under pressure he finally agreed, and included the tale of the manuscript in his essay.

Du Mu was a serious young man, and reproved Li He for exceeding the order of things ('li'), in a catalogue that begins with "A continuous stream of clouds and mist has not such a manner as his...; waters stretching far off into the distance have not such a mood as his; all spring's flowering glory has not his gentleness;" and goes on through the attributes until "the leviathan's gaping maw and the leaping sea turtle, the bull demon and the snake god, have not his sense of fantasy and illusion."

Li Shangyin read Du Mu's account of Li He's strangeness, and responded with a "Short Biography of Li He." The biographer interviewed Li's sister, and discovered a young man who excelled at both "painstaking composition and writing swiftly." Han Yu (a major figure of the transition from High to Late Tang) understood the boy who never brooded over his poems. Li He rode around on a donkey, writing poems which he threw into a bag. "When he went back in the evening," Li Shangyin reported, "his mother had a serving girl take the bag and empty its contents; when she saw how much he had written, his mother burst out with: 'This boy won't stop until he has spit out his heart.' Then she lit the lamps and gave him his dinner."

Paradoxically, the past century of scholarship devoted to opening Chinese, while often engaging and clear from moment to moment, adds up to a larger confusion. In every sense, China is just so big. It doesn't help that, over the past 40 years, the transcription conventions have changed. Ssu-ma Ch'ien is now Sima Qian. Of the High Tang poets, Li Po (Ezra Pound's Rihaku) became Li Bo, then Li Bai; Tu Fu (China's Greatest Poet) now is Du Fu; Po Chü-I passed through Bo Chü-yi to Bai Juyi; only Wang Wei has remained Wang Wei.

This shapeshifting is another instance of what Owen calls "Chineseness," a firm reminder that even the most serious and respectful English Orientalism lies close to the border of inscrutability, take-out menus, and Surrealist exquisite cadavers. In *The Great Age of Chinese Poetry*, Tai Shu-lun offers some High Tang literary advice: "The scene a poet creates is as when the sun is warm on Indigo Fields and the fine jade gives off mist: you can gaze on it, but you cannot fix it in your eyes."

Poets always think about immortality, even when they court it fecklessly, like Li He. Du Fu wrote about "a fame that lasts a thousand years." Li Po's "River Merchant's Wife" says:

> At fifteen I stopped scowling,
> I desired my dust to be mingled with yours
> Forever and forever and forever.

And manuscripts were only one way to transmit poems or to speak about poetry in those late days, before the 10th century when redactors collected poems into books and fixed the canon.

Early in the 9th Century, the poet Han Yu was asked to compose an inscription for a stone monument commemorating a military victory of his patron, Pei Du. Rivals at court thought Pei Du's role was exaggerated in the poet's account. The stele was toppled, its inscription erased and replaced with another. Yet Han Yu's celebration of the victory endured as one of his most famous works. Li Shangyin's poem "Han Yu's Stele," is written in Han Yu's voice. The poet recalls the composition and destruction of his stele in the third person. Owen cautions that the poem does not welcome translation. Yet something of its complexity, the pressure of time and desire, survive the unmusical English telling.

Here is the description of a poem's fate:

> His [Han Yu's] text that represents this Culture
> is like the Primal Essence:
> well before this it had already
> entered people's innards.
> Tang's basin and Kong's tripod
> had their inscriptions;
> we no longer have the vessels today,
> but their words have been preserved....

and here, a manifesto of poetic ambition:

> I wish to make ten thousand copies
> and recite it ten thousand times,
> saliva dripping from the mouth's corners.
> my right hand calloused.
> Pass it on for generations
> seventy and two,
> to use it in the Feng and Shan rites, jade tablets
> > and the foundation of the Hall of Light.

PLAINCLOTHES POLICEMEN OF LANGUAGE:
The Savage Detectives

Setting aside Osip Mandelstam's contention that everything a poet writes is actually a gloss on himself, no matter the topic, I normally don't write about myself. But I have an uncanny relationship with Roberto Bolaño.

Bolaño's fictions fuse the received with the imagined, the anticipated with what's remembered, politics and poetry with faith and expediency. They're at once particularized, and abuzz with the same otherworldly aura that Jorge Luis Borges generates with his scholastic visions. But where Borges, a blind man, fashions what might be termed blueprints of time, or machines that read such prints, Roberto Bolaño places poetry at the center of his enterprise.

By poetry, I understand Bolaño to mean (as I do) the only form of the human voice that lasts, which is in turn the only human thing that lasts. Everything else (insert here a complete dictionary, or better, alphabets waiting to be arranged) says goodbye as it arrives. I take pleasure, too, in the way Bolaño (like Tolstoy, Proust, Cervantes, Dickens, Borges and so forth) weaves the folk of actual history, literary and otherwise, into the lives of his characters: real readers of imaginary books, real books about imaginary people, and so on in finite but unlimited variation.

Earlier this year, I read *Distant Star* (1996/2004), which Bolaño published in Spanish before *The Savage Detectives* (1998/2007).

Nothing in my experience as a reader of strange, wrought, penetrating books of any sort prepared me for the repeated shock I felt reading *Distant Star*. Its central character is named Wieder, Carlos Wieder. First encountered in a writing workshop, Wieder later resurfaces as a Chilean Air Force Captain who sky-writes his poems, and commands a military death squad under Pinochet. Seeing my surname, not a common one, again and again, *wieder und wieder*, left me asking what I almost never ask when reading a book: Who is this writer? How does he know me?

Born in Chile in 1953, Roberto Bolaño moved to Mexico City with his family in 1968. In 1973, he returned to Chile to make a socialist nation, but the army seized power and arrested him. Bolaño went back to Mexico, moved on to Paris, and ultimately settled in Barcelona. He wrote nine novels, two books of stories and five volumes of poetry. In 1998, he was awarded the Romulo Gallegos prize for *Los detectives salvajes*. Roberto Bolaño died in 2003, aged 50, awaiting a liver transplant.

My ignorance of even canonical Spanish writing is large and longstanding. As a college student in New York in the late 1960s, with a Panamanian roommate who spent a lot of time in discotheques, I knew two sentences (both subway signs, I can't swear by my spelling): *la via del tren es peligrosa* (the way of the train is dangerous); and (*el abe que sabe vuela por Pan American*): the bird who knows flies Pan American. Latin American writers meant Borges, Garcia Marquez, Octavio Paz and Pablo Neruda. I didn't get the jokes in *Don Quixote*. Modern Spain was Picasso, Miró, Salvador Dali, Luis Bunuel, Miguel de Unamuno—and Franco, which meant fascists, who murdered Garcia Lorca. Don't forget the Spanish Inquisition.

MUSIC ART

I lived in Mallorca for a few weeks in 1975, and stopped in Madrid on the way home. Parked in a hotel across from the Prado, I spoke to no-one, passing my time with Bruegel's "The Hay Wain" and el Bosco's "The Garden of Earthly Delights." By the time Bolaño's visceral realists arrived in Europe (if *The Savage Detectives*' timeline holds true), I was back in New York City, in psychoanalysis with a Catalan Freudian named Quim, whose anarchist brother had been executed under Franco.

In 2006, I responded to a constellation of forces—the study of Arabic, a new *Zohar* translation, ditto *Don Quixote*, restlessness. Medieval Jewish and Arabic poetry and philosophy are a repressed memory, not just mine. My wife and I took a plane to Spain. We travelled through Andalusia: Seville, Cadiz, Ronda, Malaga, Granada. Then via Garcia Lorca Airport, I returned to Catalonia, to Barcelona.

The Savage Detectives is arranged in three parts: The first and third, "Mexicans Lost in Mexico (1975)" and "The Sonora Desert (1996)," are the journal of a 17-year-old first-year law student and poet, Juan Garcia Madero. His daily entries for the last two months of 1975, and then January-February 1976, bracket "The Savage Detectives (1976-1996)." This middle section, the novel *per se*, might be over-simply described as an oral history of the Mexican visceral realists, compiled between 1976 and 1996, as gathered through the recollections (or are they affidavits?) of individuals who crossed paths or purposes with the leaders of the movement's second wave, Ulisses Lima and Arturo Belano.

"The Savage Detectives" divides into 26 chapters (one for each letter of the alphabet). The story, or mystery, is told in the Mexico

POETRY HISTORY

City rooms of Amadeo Salvatierra, near the Palacio de la Inquisición, over one long night in January, 1976.

Salvatierra, a minor figure associated with both the Mexican Stridentists and the visceral realists of the 1920s, supports himself as a scribe. He answers the inquiries of those he calls "three boys" into the life and poems of Cesárea Tinajero, mother of visceral realism. "Who is Cesárea Tinajero?" is one mystery pursued by The Savage Detectives. But who are the three boys? Probably Belano and Lima, but who is the third? Are they the detectives? What is a poet without poems? Is not having an answer the same as there being no answer? Is disappearing the same as dying? Why do we do what we do, and does it matter?

Over his last bottle of Los Suicidas mezcal—no longer available in stores—Amadeo Salvatierra recalls events of 40, 50 years past, and his oral history ripples outward, forward across two decades and five continents. In each of the 26 chapters, the multiple narrators are also characters, engines of the plot: poets and painters, novelists, critics, architects, anthropologists, editors, publishers, drug dealers, whores, pimps and gangsters, lawyers and heiresses, nazis and kabbalists, body-builders, lottery winners and Mexican Jews brought together like the thieves in *The Maltese Falcon*, in a quest for poetry.

Midway through the evening and the book, one of the three boys asks Salvatierra, "Where are Cesárea Tinajero's poems?" The scribe digs out the sole surviving copy of the only issue of *Caborca*, and shows them Cesárea's one poem: "Sión." The poem can't be quoted: it's a visual stack of three drawings. They depict (from top to bottom) a small rectangle on top of a straight line; a small rectangle on one slope of a wavy line; a small rectangle on the steep of a jagged line. Salvatierra then asked the boys what they made of this poem, which he'd been looking at for more than forty years and "never understood a goddamn thing." They answer, that the poem's a joke covering up something more serious. The scribe still wants to know what it means. They think. Time passes. They talk about other pieces in *Caborca*. "Well, then, I said, what's the mystery? Then the boys looked at me and said: there is no mystery, Amadeo."

In "Mexicans Lost in Mexico," the December 14 entry in García Madero's journal records that no one gives the visceral realists ANYTHING (his caps), meaning money, column inches, invitations to party or to read. "Belano and Lima" he notes, "are like two ghosts." Then he asks: "If *simón* is slang for yes and *nel* means no, then what does *simonel* mean?"

Amadeo Salvatierra dispatches the detectives to interview Manuel Maple Arce, translator of John Dos Passos (really) and friend of Borges (maybe). The old man observes that "all poets, even the most avant-garde, need a father. But these poets were meant to be orphans."

According to Quim Font, institutionalized Catalan architect, visceral realist magazine designer, father of the wildest girl in Mexico City and unshakeable reality principle, Belano and Lima are writers of desperate poems. This limits their appeal, because desperate poems require desperate readers.

All second generation visceral realist poems are allusions, never citations. The only evidence of their existence is the memory of others. This is the contrapositive of Mandelstam's poetry, which was only preserved because others memorized it, and a variation on the Borgesian conceit that no book exists until a book is written about it.

In the case of Belano and Lima, their very existence depends upon others' memories. For good or ill:

A Latin-spouting Galician lawyer puts his money in a Barcelona poetry magazine. He thinks he is a poet, a giant. Then he finds Belano (a nobody) in bed with his daughter.

A Chilean bar owner in Barcelona recounts his tale of amazing luck. This multiple lottery winner addresses Belano directly, implying that the writer is present at the transcription, if not the scribe himself.

Octavio Paz's secretary remembers a literary encounter between Paz and Ulisses Lima in a seedy Mexico City park.

"The Sonora Desert" picks up Garcia Madero's journal on New Year's Day, 1976. The quest for Cesárea Tinajero ends in a fatal duel in the dust. Idling in the the bordertown of Villaviciosa, the journalist's imagination gives out. The last entry is a line-drawing riddle.

In Chapter 26 of "The Savage Detectives," Professor Ernesto Garcia Grajales of Pachuca describes himself in December, 1996, as "the only expert on the visceral realists in Mexico, and if pressed, the world." Grajales delivers an epilogue, a "where are they now?" of Bolaño's epic cast, the living and the dead. The Professor never heard of Juan Garcia Madero, and categorically denies that he belonged to the group. Taking his leave, he observes that "there are labyrinths I prefer not to lose myself in....Let readers and scholars draw their own conclusions."

MUSIC ART

The last word goes to Amadeo Salvatierra. Disturbed when one of the three boys talking in his sleep promises to find the Complete Works of Cesárea Tinajero, the old scribe looks at the walls of his front room, at "my books, my photographs, the stains on the ceiling, and then I looked at them and I saw them as if through a window, one of them with his eyes open and the other with his eyes shut, but both of them looking, looking out? looking in? I don't know, all I know is that their faces had turned pale, as if they were at the North Pole, and I told them so, and the one who was sleeping breathed noisily and said: it's more as if the North Pole had descended on Mexico City, that's what he said, and I asked: boys, are you cold? a rhetorical question, or a practical question, because if the answer was yes, I was determined to make them coffee right away, but ultimately it was really a rhetorical question, if they were cold all they had to do was move away from the window, and then I said: boys, is it worth it? is it worth it? is it really worth it? and then one who was asleep said *Simonel....*"

MUSIC ART

WHEN MILTON SAYS 'SING'

John Milton recently passed his 400th birthday.

I wouldn't recommend Milton's sacred epics, or even his short poems, to a newcomer to the English language. Andrew Marvell, John Donne, William Blake, and Emily Dickinson share his themes, are good to learn by heart, and can be entered through many gates. They write in the vernacular, maybe encrusted by the fashions of their times, but still alluring. Adamantine, hard from the start, Milton's English poetry aspires to Biblical Hebrew and, for good or ill, succeeds.

Milton is read mostly in university courses (that's by the priestly caste) and by novelists and poets. Unlike the Bible, or Blake, or Dickinson, *Paradise Lost* is not amenable to paraphrase. There's no graphic novelization, no stage or movie treatment even of his life, much less of the (relatively) simple *Paradise Regain'd*. The greatness of his art is its difficulty, its intransigence, its irreducible material. All Milton's settings and actions occur in the mind. Even *Samson Agonistes*, patterned on Greek tragedy, was not intended for performance. Whatever the virtues of the Handel oratorio based on Milton's text, it is something other, and less, than the original.

Paradise Lost, *Paradise Regain'd*, and *Samson Agonistes* were dictated by a blind poet, they were not written. When Milton says "Sing," he's invoking more than literary convention. He couldn't proof his last works, never saw the books in print or read them to himself. Unless the epics are read aloud, it's impossible to hear them, no matter how developed the inward ear. This presents a daunting task for a generation taught to read to itself without moving the lips. But it's the basic requirement for a reader (or at least for me) to discover what one thought one knew but does not know.

The pressure of speaking about events and forces prior to language required Milton to straddle both sides, to admit the impossibility of what he attempted and still do it. He includes everything he knows, throws everything in to his poems, everything he can remember. Memory is the mother of the Muses. It's also the second duty enjoined by the Hebrew Bible ("Hear, O Israel" would be the first.)

Learning may be a prerequisite to reading John Milton's poetry, but that learning is not impossible. The poems were not opaque to his contemporaries, who shared an English education, urgent political choices, and pre-messianic unease. The iambic pentameter metronome ticking inside the head of a renaissance reader kept time for the first line of Paradise Lost, "Of man's first disobedience, and the fruit," and marked disobedience's metrical betrayal. Likewise, an auditor of the fallen angels' council and debates in Hell did not require academic commentary to connect either the defiant spirit in defeat, or the perils of despair, with the recent Rebellion, Cromwell's Protectorate, and the Stuart Restoration. It was an age when even theology had consequences.

Creation, The War in Heaven, Chaos, Sin and Death, Satan, Adam and Eve in the Garden and their Fall, Redemption: even the grandest and remotest of Milton's themes is informed by intimacy struggling with diffidence and guilt. Adam's passionate attachment to and disappointment in Eve banks the embers of Milton's three marriages. Jesus' renunciation of gentile poetry and philosophy in *Paradise Regain'd* must have tasted strange in the mouth of the classical scholar. Then there's that howl, Samson lamenting his blindness:

> O dark, dark, dark, amid the blaze of noon,
> Irrecoverably dark, total Eclipse
> Without all hope of day!

Coming from anyone else, these lines might be bombast. From the lips of one "with mortal voice, unchang'd/ To hoarce or mute, though fall'n on evil dayes,/ On evil dayes though fall'n, and evil tongues;/ In darkness, and with dangers compast round,/ And solitude..." they are overdetermined: too, too true.

It's tempting to think of Milton as all learning and intensity, with no nature. His Cambridge classmates dubbed their long-haired, sober scholar "Our Lady of Christ's College." And from youth, the poet devoted himself to what he only got around to accomplishing in the last decades of his life: writing a sacred epic that reconciles the course of divine history with the journey of the solitary soul. In the last fifteen years of his life, Milton openly proclaimed himself an anointed prophet. It was 2000 years after the destruction of Solomon's Temple, when prophecy ceased in Israel. The pagan oracles fell silent at Jesus' birth. Such large claims, and his conviction that he possessed an upright heart, and pure, however honestly come by, do nothing to soften resistance. The man and his works seem indissoluble, with the density and gravity of matter.

In 1673, one year before his death, Milton added his translation from the Latin of "The Fifth Ode of Horace, Book I" to the last edition of his minor poems. Here's the whole thing:

> What slender Youth bedew'd with liquid odours
> > Courts thee on Roses in some pleasant Cave,
> > *Pyrrha* for whom bindst thou
> > In wreaths thy golden Hair,
>
> Plain in thy neatness; O how oft shall he
> > On Faith and changed Gods complain: and Seas
> > Rough with black winds and storms
> > Unwonted shall admire:
>
> Who now enjoyes thee credulous, all Gold,
> > Who always vacant, always amiable
> > Hopes thee; of flattering gales
> > Unmindfull. Hapless they
>
> To whom thou untry'd seem'st fair. Me in my vow'd
> > Picture the sacred wall declares t' have hung
> > My dank and dropping weeds
> > To the stern God of Sea.

The first half of this sixteen line poem asks series of questions without question marks:

"What slender Youth bedew'd with liquid odours/ Courts thee..."; "O how oft shall he/...complain"–the "thee" being Pyrrha, erotic other with golden hair.

But the thought doesn't stop there. Milton's sentence continues through line twelve: "Who now enjoys thee.../ Who alwayes vacant, alwayes amiable/ Hopes thee..."

Depending on where the reader-aloud stresses the "whos," who can be heard as "he who," enjoying present bliss; or as "who?" the poet remembering love now disenchanted. This cuts-both-ways, all-purpose love lyric (in English) belongs to the same tradition as Ben Jonson's tavern song with Latin roots, "To Celia" ("Drink to me, onely, with thine eyes,") which can be delivered, depending on where the stress falls, as a blessing or a curse. Up to line 12, the Ode is a comrade also to the urbane, disenchanted John Donne of "Go, and catch a falling star…"

But where men of tarnished hopes distance themselves through knowingness or doubleness or irony, Milton's lover takes a different turn: "Hapless they/ To whom thou untry'd seemst fair." Pyrrha's beauty, real or illusive, must be tried, or nothing happens: no desire, guilt, or virtue.

I have no idea about the last sentence, those last four lines, which I can't parse, or assemble, yet unnerve me nonetheless.

AVATARS OF TRUE FEELING: *The Ramayana of Valmiki*

The *Ramayana of Valmiki* is the oldest Sanskrit epic. Over seven books and some 50,000 lines, the poem celebrates the life of Rama, incarnation of Vishnu, founder of the Golden Age, peerless warrior, master of scripture, obedient son and exemplary brother, dedicated lover and husband of Sita, daughter of the Earth.

Valmiki composed his holy story of Rama and Sita sometime between the seventh and fourth centuries before the Common Era. That makes his poem younger than Hesiod's *Theogony* and Homer's *Iliad* and *Odyssey*, but roughly contemporaneous with writings of the Hebrew Prophets, Gautama Buddha, Confucius, Herodotus, Aeschylus, and Plato.

Nothing is hidden. Sacred legend, the struggle between good and evil, divine intention and human ambition, the cross-currents of personal obligation and right conduct, and the possibility of happiness, all unfurl in a work meant to be both read and performed. The *Ramayana* informs, enlightens and entrances, even in translation.

Balakanda, or *Boyhood*, Book One of the epic's seven books, tells the story of the Ramayana's own conception in its first four cantos. It also tells the history of Rama at least two ways, before the actual events unfold. Throughout, Valmiki's poem vibrates between heightened self-awareness and rapture.

Canto 1 opens with Valmiki asking the sage Narada: "Is there a man in the world today who is truly virtuous?"

The sage responds that there lives a man named Rama. He then relates what might be called Rama's official history, from princely birth, exile, and martial triumphs, ending with the golden age.

After he heard Rama's story, Valmiki went down to the riverbank to bathe. There, he saw a Nisháda hunter kill the male of a pair of *krauñcha* birds. Filled with grief at this injustice, the ascetic said: "Since, Nisháda, you killed one of this pair of *krauñchas*, distracted at the height of passion, you shall not live for very long." But even as he spoke, the compassionate sage wondered what this was which he had uttered. Upon reflection, Valmiki decided that this utterance, fixed in metrical quarters, each with the same 32 syllables, "produced in this access of *shoka*, grief, shall be called *shloka*, poetry, and nothing else."

Next, Brahma, the maker of worlds, visited Valmiki, and informed him that it was by the god's will alone that the poet produced his *shloka*, his elegant speech. Brahma then commanded Valmiki to compose the entire history of Rama as he heard it from Naráda, "the full story, public and private.... For all that befell... will be revealed to you, even those events of which you are ignorant. No utterance of yours in this poem shall be false."

In the days after Rama had regained his kingdom, the seer Valmiki composed the whole *Ramayana*. Its episodes, as rehearsed in Canto 3, include the future and final events which had not yet befallen Rama on earth.

But who would perform this story of Sita and the slaying of Ravana which is "sweet both when recited and when sung..., eminently suitable for the accompaniment of both stringed and percussion instruments"?

In Canto 4, the youths Kusha and Lava become Valmiki's students, and learn the entire *Ramayana* by heart. Gifted musicians, they sing the poem with such single-minded concentration before assemblies of seers, brahmans and good men, that its events seemed to be happening before their eyes.

Valmiki's two disciples are brothers, princes, Rama's sons by Sita. They do not know their father. Rama, in turn, is unaware of their existence. Yet the fame of their performance reached royal Rama's household. So the king brought the singers to his home and, turning to his own brothers Lakshmana, Shatru·ghna, and Bharata, said:

> "'Let us listen to this tale, whose words and meaning alike are wonderful.... Moreover, it is said that this profound tale they tell is highly beneficial, even for me. Listen to it.'
>
> "Then, at a word from Rama,..." Kusha and Lava "began to sing in the full perfection of the *marga* mode. And right there in the assembly, even Rama, in his desire to experience it fully, gradually permitted his mind to become enthralled." (1.4.25-29)

Whatever its historical date of composition, the *Ramayana* was written in early days of Rama's regained kingdom, which places Valmiki's discovery of poetry at the end of *Yuddhakāṇḍa*, Book Six in the epic chronology.

Yuddhakāṇḍa, the sixth of seven planned volumes from the Ramayana Translation Project, has just been published by Princeton University Press. *Yuddhakāṇḍa* sings the war of annihilation between the forces of good and evil. Led by Rama and his brother

Lakshmana, the massed armies of the monkey King Sugriva and the hero Hanuman cross the ocean from the mainland to Lanka, capital of the ten-headed *rakshasa* king Ravana. They destroy the evil demon's kingdom and reunite the abducted Sita with Rama. Rama returns home after his 14-year exile, reclaims his throne, and ushers in the Golden Age.

The longest book in Valmiki's epic, *Yuddhakāṇḍa* unfolds over 116 *sargas*. They fill 376 pages in translators Robert Goldman, Sally Sutherland Goldman and Barend van Nooten's stanza-spaced, numbered prose verses. The Englished *shlokas*, with their carefully-pointed romanized Sanskrit words where English will not serve, look like a kind of poetry which disregards the customary rules, yet summons the need to understand rather than the impulse to correct.

An 118-page scholarly introduction and 1161 octavo pages of back-matter annotations, bibliography, glossary and index support, but don't intrude upon, the body of the text. The introduction takes up matters of meaning, theme and character, style and structure, commentary and translation. There's even a discussion of *Yuddhakāṇḍa* cinematic qualities. The extensive annotation considers variant passages. It clarifies such details as the identity of beings, weapons and creatures which retain their Sanskrit names in the translation. For example, the *hamsa* is a bar-headed goose, Mute swan, or Whooper swan; and the *sārasa* is the Indian sarus crane.

The first five volumes of this translation of the *Ramayana* are also available from the Clay Sanskrit Library. Easier to come by than the Princeton versions, the Clay editions are bi-lingual, a Sanskrit version of the Loeb Classical Library. Addressed to Sanskrit students, these sextodecimo books eschew big scholarly apparatus. A brief introduction and guides to pronunciation and punctuation precede the romanized, transliterated Sanskrit verse with facing translation. Unlike the scholarly edition, the Clay Library sets its English text as prose. Marginal numbers synchronize the paragraphs with the corresponding Sanskrit *shlokas*. Each volume ends with a glossary and index.

Without the formality of verse blocks, the same translation reads like a narrative. There are other differences. The Clay volumes go by plain English or simplified rather than full Sanskrit titles. The forthcoming Princeton University Press edition *Volume VII: Uttarakanda* will appear in the bi-lingual Clay Sanskrit Library edition as *The Final Chapter*. Also, the orthographic rigors of the Princeton edition are dropped. The plainer Clay format transcribes *Śloka* as *shloka*; *rakṣasa* is spelled *rakshasa*; *kāṇḍa* and *sarga* become book and canto.

The pleasures of Sanskrit-verse-in-English take some getting used to. Elegantly mannered and rhetorically extravagant, it possesses gravity and expressive breadth, and profound credibility. Profusion of detail and address informs every line like a creative principle, a force of nature.

The *Yuddhakāṇḍa* opens with Rama prey to the despondence he's felt since the day back in Book Three, *The Forest,* when Ravana abducted Sita from their ashram in exile. Now, in the second *sarga* of Book Six, Rama's ally Sugriva the monkey king, asks:

"'Why do you grieve, hero, like some other, ordinary man?

Don't be like that! Abandon your grief, as an ingrate does friendship."'

Despite Sugriva's urgings that he recall himself and lead Hanuman and the vast monkey army across the ocean to Lanka where Sita's held captive, Rama laments to his brother, Lakshmana:

> "'They say that grief diminishes with the passage of time. But bereft as I am of the sight of my beloved, mine only increases day by day.
>
> "'I do not suffer because my beloved is so far away, nor even because she has been abducted. This alone is the source of all my grief: her youth is slipping away.
>
> "'Blow, breeze, where my beloved stays. Touch her and then touch me. For the touching of our limbs now depends on you, as on the moon depends the meeting of our glances.'" (6:5:4-6)

The greater part of *Yuddhakāṇḍa* consists of battle scenes of a visual and auditory intensity very different in kind from the earth-bound pitched battles in the *Iliad*, or Herodotus' descriptions of Xerxes' armies. Consider the crescendo-decrescendo and hot-to-cold flashing of this confrontation, with its shifting perspective:

> 'Then, in that terrible darkness, the frenzied *rakshasas* attacked Rama with hails of arrows.
>
> 'And the uproar that they made as they rushed upon him, roaring in fury, was like the sound of the upheaval of the seven seas at the time of universal destruction....
>
> 'Pierced in every vital point by Rama with his hail of arrows, they crawled away from the battle, barely clinging to life.

'Then mighty Rama illuminated all directions with his arrows which, with their shafts adorned with gold, resembled flames of fire.

'As for the remaining *rakshasa* heroes who stood their ground before Rama, they, too, were destroyed, like moths entering a flame.

'With thousands of arrows flying, their feathers fletched with gold, the night was as lovely as an autumnal evening sparkling with fireflies.' (6.34.16-23)

This poetry of elaboration and profusion turns the common ancestry of bow and stringed instruments into a mortal concert, marrying æsthetic splendor to horror and pathos:

'With the twanging of bowstrings in place of the sweet sound of the lute, the gasps of the dying for the beating of time, and the faint cries of the wounded in place of singing, the battle resembled a musical recital.' (6.42.23)

Typically, the *Ramayana* describes the troops waging this war between the monkeys and the *rakshasa* hosts in millions and billions. In time the large numbers, like the chilly distances of astronomy or the vaporous magnitudes of plutocrats and economists, beggar understanding and numb pity. Homer particularized his warriors, granting even walk-on combatants a unique history, distinction, and anatomically explicit death. Or he imagined sublime unequal single combat, like Achilles fighting with the river Skamander outside the walls of Troy. Valmiki celebrates the battle for Lanka as a conflict of race against race, so vast it needs four *shlokas* to anatomize the undifferentiated legions who feed the maw:

'Indeed, the battleground resembled a river. Masses of slain heroes formed its banks, and shattered weapons, its great trees. Torrents of blood made up its broad waters, and the ocean to which it flowed was Yama. Livers and spleens made up its deep mud, scattered entrails its waterweeds. Severed heads and trunks made up its fish, pieces of limbs, its grass. It was crowded with vultures in place of flocks of *haṃsas*, and it was swarming with adjutant storks instead of *sārasa* cranes. It was covered with fat in place of foam, and the cries of the wounded took the place of its gurgling. It was not to be forded by the faint of heart. Truly, it resembled a river at the end of the rains, swarming with *haṃsas* and *sārasa* cranes.' (6.46.25-28)

The hyperbolic sublime also has its droll moments.

In *Sarga* 48, Ravana sends an army to awaken the enormous *rakshasa* Kumbhakarna, who is addicted to sleep. Over forty *shlokas*, the hard-put delegates of the ten-necked demon king try to arouse the sleeper first with piles of meat, then with pots of blood and strong drink. They smear him with sandalpaste, utter praises and roaring. They blow conches, clap their arms, belabor the giant with bludgeons and cudgels and maces, but they cannot withstand the wind from his snoring. They beat drums, they drive horses, camels, donkeys and elephants over him;

> '...finally, when they made a thousand elephants trample across his body, Kumbhakarna, aware of a slight sensation, at last awoke.
>
> 'Ignoring the tremendous blows of mountaintops and trees that were being hurled down upon him, he suddenly leapt

up at the violent interruption of his sleep, yawning and oppressed by fear and hunger.

'Stretching wide his arms, which were as strong as mountain peaks and resembled two mountain peaks or great serpents, that night-roaming *rakshasa* yawned grotesquely, opening his mouth, which was like a gaping mare's head fire that lies beneath the sea.

'And as he yawned prodigiously, his mouth, as wide as the underworld Patala, resembled the sun, maker of day, risen over the summit of Mount Meru.

'Yawning, the enormously powerful night-roaming *rakshasa* was at last fully awake. His breath was like a gale from the mountains.' (6:48:47-51)

Having slain Ravana, granted him a funeral, and consecrated the demon's brother Vibhisana as the new king of Lanka, Rama dispatched Hanuman to Ravana's palace with a message for Sita. "Inform her," Rama commanded, "that Sugriva, Lakshmana and I are well, and that I have slain Ravana.... Please take a message from her and return."

To this embassy Sita responded, "Foremost of monkeys, I wish to see my husband."

Her reply plunged Rama into gloom. Staring at the ground, he ordered that Sita be washed and adorned and brought before him, although she would have preferred to appear before him as the rescued captive. Instead, surrounded by hosts of his friends, Rama received his wife:

"'So here you are, my good woman. I have won you back after conquering my enemy in battle. Whatever there was to be done through manly valor, I have now accomplished....

"'I have wiped clean the affront, and so my wrath is appeased. For I have eliminated both the insult and my enemy at the same time.

"'Today... I am once more master of myself.'"

'As Rama was saying these words in that fashion, Sita, wide-eyed like a doe, was overcome with tears.

'But as Rama gazed upon her, his anger flared up once more, like the raging flame of a fire drenched with melted butter....

"'In wiping away this affront, Sita, I have accomplished all that a man could do....

"'Bless you, but it was not on your account that I undertook this war...

"'Instead, I did all this in order to protect my reputation...

"'Since, however, your virtue is now in doubt, your presence has become as profoundly disagreeable to me as is a bright lamp to a man afflicted with a disease of the eye.

"'Go, therefore, as you please, daughter of Janaka. You have my permission. Here are the ten directions. I have no further use for you, my good woman.

"'For what powerful man born in a respectable family—his heart tinged with affection—would take back a woman who had lived in the house of another man?'" (103:2-19)

Sita bade Lakshmana build a pyre. She circled Rama, bowed to the gods and brahmans, declared her purity, and "As Sita entered the fire, a deafening and prodigious cry of 'Alas! Alas!' arose from the *rakshasas* and monkeys."

The gods flew to Lanka in their chariots, and Brahma asked Rama, "How can you, the creator of the entire universe, the most ancient one, and foremost among those possessing supreme knowledge, stand by and watch as Sita falls into the fire, eater of oblations? How can you not realize that you are foremost among the hosts of the gods?"

To which Rama replied, "I think of myself only as a man, Rama, the son of Dasaratha. May the Blessed Lord please tell me who I really am, to whom I belong, and why I am here?"

For all the monkeys, vultures, divine beings, demons, and gods swirling through the Ramayana, only Rama and Sita count as avatars of true feeling. Married, peerless, loving and devoted to the practice of righteousness, power, and pleasure, neither will ever know another partner. Separated twice—once by Ravana to incite a holy war, and once by Rama's decision to embrace the burden of sovereignty as will be recounted in Book Seven—the monogamous pair make a strong case for mortal unhappiness.

The *Ramayana* has generated literary spin-offs and reimaginings for 1500 years at least. In the 7th-century, the poet Bhatti wrote *The Death of Ravana*, a retelling of Rama's story that teaches classical Sanskrit grammar without a textbook. *Rama's Last Act*, an early 8th century CE Sanskrit play by Bhava·bhuti, dramatizes the events of

Uttarakāṇḍa. Murari's play *Rama Beyond Price*, is a seven-act remake of Valmiki's poem that closes with the triumphs of *Yuddhakāṇḍa* minus the trial by fire, and a happy ending. All three works are available in the Clay Sanskrit series.

An illustrated *Ramayana* commissioned by mid-17th-century Rajasthani ruler Jagat Singh has been reproduced by the British Library, with 128 color plates. The manuscript makes a pictorial narrative of Valmiki's poem. There's a book-by-book plot summary, and running captions identify the episodes depicted. Of course, visual imagination stands in the stead of poetry.

In Valmiki's world, poetry is the highest form of discourse: a measured utterance capable of simultaneous ecstasy and cognition. Poetry is "replete with all the poetic sentiments: the humorous, the erotic, the piteous, the wrathful, the heroic, the terrifying, the loathsome and the rest." How else could it speak truly of the human? How else to come to terms with this world?

Decorous, extravagant, true if not history, who could dismiss as rhetoric Valmiki's sacred hyperbole? "Whoever reads this history of Rama, which is purifying, destructive of sin, holy and the equal of the Vedas, is freed from all sin. A man who reads this *Ramáyana* story, which leads to long life, will after death rejoice in heaven together with his sons, grandsons and attendants. A brahman who reads it becomes eloquent, a *kshátriya* becomes a lord of the earth, a *vaishya* acquires profit from his goods, and even a lowly *shudra* achieves greatness."

AN OLD MAN: *Taoteching*

When prose confronts the ineffable, the discussion or explanation can leave a person thinking that, because it's been discussed or explained, he understands.

Poetry, on the other hand, is at once immediate and cryptic, a cry which defies explanation—one thing poetry shares with a good joke. That, and the ability to inspire unease.

All the Chinese sages except Lao-tzu spoke in prose. Lao-tzu's *Taoteching* is a book of poems about the *Tao* (the Way), and *te* (Virtue, the Way in action). The book's 81 verses or chapters employ by one count 28 different kinds of rhyme. Its classical Chinese characters, which are brush-stroke pictographs independent of dialect, admit of variant and or simultaneous interpretations.

Lao-tzu's manual of self-cultivation and self-defense perched between knowing and unknowing has held sway for over 2500 years. Only the Hebrew Bible (set down by many hands) and the *Bhagavad Gita* (one episode in an anonymous oral Sanskrit epic) have been translated more often. The Bible and the *Gita* reveal and elaborate what happens in the light, and are reconciled to, if not happy with, both duty and mortality. The *Taoteching* espouses detachment, embraces darkness, and addresses the solitary self before the social being. Lao-tzu treats long life as an end unto itself, and through selflessness espouses immortality, an end with no end.

A tall order for any translator.

As a man without Chinese, I'd love to have some idea of, some English analogy for, how Lao-tzu's poetry works. Sticking to those who wrote short, does the old sage sound like John Donne off the pulpit, Blake without the devil, or Emily Dickinson in Asia?

Lao-tzu wrote the *Taoteching* during the sixth century before the common era. He was already an old man when, according to Ssu-ma Ch'ien's *Records of The Grand Historian of China,* the young Confucius sought him out. The elder prefaced his remarks to the younger by observing that "the ancients you admire have been in the ground a long time. Their bones have turned to dust. Only their words remain."

Confucius and the later sages (who are ancients to us) left annals, aphorisms, tales, persuasions moral and politic, parables and paradoxes. Even in translation, their writings have a gravity and magnetic tone akin to music, prose being the music of the fallen.

Here, for example, is a passage from Irene Bloom's new edition of Mencius, a Confucian sage who lived about two centuries after Lao-tzu:

> Mencius says, "It once was that the worthy would, through their own enlightenment, cause others to be enlightened. Now, there are those who try through their own benightedness to enlighten others."

Mencius is the sage of the possible; Lao-tzu is the poet of the Dark Union. *Taoteching* verse 56, begins: "Those who know don't talk/ those who talk don't know." Answering and unanswerable, Lao-tzu sometimes said things for the sake of the rhyme, an sign not that the sage wrote doggerel, but that his imperative is as much formal and musical as moral and philosophical.

Verse six of the *Taoteching* is one of the few poems that's been transmitted without significant variants through tens of centuries of Chinese editions. James Legge's monumental translation of the Chinese Classics from the late 19th century renders it in rhymed couplets:

> The valley spirit dies not, aye the same;
> The female mystery thus do we name.
> Its gate, from which at first they issued forth,
> Is called the root from which grew heaven and earth.
> Long and unbroken does its power remain,
> Used gently, and without the touch of pain.

Nearly one-hundred years later, Robert Henricks translates the same poem in simple prose, arranged in lines:

> The valley spirit never dies;
> We call it the mysterious female.
> The gates of the mysterious female–
> These we call the roots of Heaven and Earth.
> Subtle yet everlasting! It seems to exist.
> In being used, it is not exhausted.

Jonathan Star's 21st-century *Tao Te Ching: The Definitive Edition*, couples a literary version of each poem with a verbatim translation-in-the-form-of-a-spreadsheet, which displays every possible meaning for each Chinese character in every poem. Star takes 19 lines to spin out verse 6. It concludes:

> Tao is limitless, unborn, eternal—
> It can only be reached through the Hidden Creator
> She is the very face of the Absolute
> The gate to the source of all things eternal
>
> Listen to Her voice
> Hear it echo through creation
> Without fail, She reveals her presence
> Without fail, She brings us to our own perfection.

Red Pine's revised edition of the *Taoteching* places each of Lao-tzu's 81 poems on a two-page spread. On the verso, the translator prints his English version alongside and to the right of the Chinese. Below the poetry and continuing on the right-hand page, he presents selections from over two millennia-worth of Chinese commentary, sometimes supplemented by his own textual observations, such as the 'valley spirit' is the moon. His sixth reads:

> The valley spirit that doesn't die
> we call the dark womb
> the dark womb's mouth
> we call the source of heaven and earth
> as elusive as gossamer silk
> and yet it can't be exhausted

And, from the accompanying commentary:

> The *Shanhaiching* says, "The Valley Spirit of the Morning Light is a black and yellow, eight-footed, eight-tailed, eight-headed animal with a human face..."

> Hsueh Hui says, "The words Lao-tzu chooses are often determined by the demands of rhyme and should not be restricted to their primary meaning. Thus, *p'in* [female animal] can also be read *p'in* [womb]."
>
> Sung Ch'ang-hsing says, "The valley spirit, the dark womb, the source of Heaven and Earth all act without acting. That we don't see them doesn't mean they don't exist."
>
> Tu Tao-chien says, "This verse also appears in *Lieh-tzu: 1.1*, where it is attributed to the Yellow Emperor instead of Lao-tzu. Lao-tzu frequently incorporates passages from ancient texts. We see their traces in 'thus the sage proclaims' or 'hence the ancients say'. Thus Confucius said, 'I don't create. I only relate.'"
>
> Lieh-tzu says, "What creates life is not itself alive."

Any book or scroll that lasts more than a thousand years has attained what passes among the living for immortality. Red Pine recalls a graduate-student moment nearly forty years ago, when the professor warned that it was time for a Sinologist to retire when he announced he was working on a new translation of the *Taoteching*. Unless, of course, the new version really is poetry. At least Red Pine's verse suggests direct speech, if not the immediacy of a stand-alone poem in English. Lucidity may not be the same thing as poetry, but it is often the next best.

The introduction to this *Taoteching* is an unequivocal pleasure. Red Pine lived many years in China, and walked the taoist landscape as well as studied its geography, history, philosophy and letters. Informed and easy, Red Pine's prose interweaves the transmission of

Lao-tzu's text and its place in Chinese culture with a personal narrative. And he manages to measure out as as much of Lao-tzu's biography as is known, ending with the sage's disappearance into anonymity in the mountains of the west. The account of Lao-tzu's meeting with Confucius, which was omitted from Burton Watson's translation of Ssu-ma Ch'ien, was a first for me. The backmatter glossary lists and illuminates proper names and Chinese terms; it gives the brief bios and dates of all the commentators and sources of the selected quotations. This dispels much strangeness attached to who, what, where and when.

    About the Tao, less said. But of the commentary, I have to ask:

    Does Huang Yuan-chi really say, "A person who can adjust their light..."?

    Do these sentences belong to Sung Ch'ang-hsing: "Doors refer to a person's mouth and nose. Windows refer to their ears and eyes..."?

    Chuang-tzu may be elusive and cryptic, but to have him teach that "Who takes Heaven as their ancestor, Virtue as their home, the Tao as their door, and who escapes change is a sage..." suggests the sage has been confused.

    Chiao Hung wonders, "If someone has no life, how can they be killed?"

    Bad grammar will kill someone, if all that's left of them, or him, is words.

TURKISH CLASSIC: Çelebi's *Book of Travels*

Evliya Çelebi's *Book of Travels* is too long to translate, and too big to write about.

Travelogue, ethnography, architectural and musical guide, dream diary and action drama, intimate portrait of the Ottoman Porte, foreign phrase book and economic catalogue, diplomatic history, it features battles and shipwrecks, deceit, escapes, wonder tales of dervishes and magicians, sexual customs and sample menus, landscape and weather, surgical practices, science, superstition and beliefs, employing an enormous 17th-century Turkish vocabulary. The *Seyahatname*'s ten volumes run to over 4300 pages in the authoritative Turkish edition.

The *Travels* made its own long journey into print. Evliya Çelebi settled in Cairo the mid-1670s for the last decade or so of his life, and finished his memoirs by 1683. The manuscript was first read in 1742, when it was transported to Istanbul and copied. It took over a century and a half for a complete, printed *Seyahatname* to appear, and that edition was as long in the press (1896-1938) as Çelebi was on the road. Most Turkish readers know the *Travels* in that version, or in condensed translation in modern Turkish. The authoritative, unbowdlerized, and corrected *Book of Travels* in the language of its composition was published between 1999 and 2007.

Çelebi's path into English also has that hint of romance. Around 1804, a German-English aristocrat, Joseph von Hammer, ran across a manuscript of volumes 1 through 4. Thinking he had the whole work in hand, Hammer issued excerpts in German translation starting in 1814. Between 1834 and 1850, he released his abbreviated English version of volumes 1 and 2: *Narrative Of Travels in Europe, Asia, and Africa, in The Seventeenth Century*, by Evliya Efendi, translated from the Turkish by the Ritter Joseph Von Hammer. That, plus a mid-20th-century version of Hammer's translation titled *In the Days of the Janissaries: Old Turkish Life as Depicted in the "Travel Book" of Evliyá Chelebí*, and a scholarly monograph, *Turkish Instruments of Music in the Seventeenth Century, as described in the Siyāḥat nāma of Ewliyā Chelebi* (extracted from the catalogue of Istanbul guilds in Volume 1) was all the English common reader had of *The Book of Travels*.

No more.

In the early 1990s, Robert Dankoff collaged a biography, *The Intimate Life of an Ottoman Statesman: Melek Ahmed Pasha (1588-1662), as Portrayed in Evliya Çelebi's Seyahatname* using von Hammer's English and the 1896-1938 Turkish. In 2010, Dankoff (an editor of the 21st-century Turkish edition) and his co-translator Sooyong Kim issued the anthology *An Ottoman Traveller: Selections from the* Book of Travels *by Evliya Çelebi*. Unlike the topical *Evliya Chelebi: Travels in Iran and the Caucasus, 1647 & 1654*, published that same year but aimed at Persian specialists, *An Ottoman Traveller* draws from all ten volumes, and gives some metonymous measure of the whole work's greatness.

The Book of Travels resembles Robert Burton's *Anatomy of Melancholy* in its exhaustive accumulation of detail; it's also akin to Herodotus' *Histories*, but picaresque. As a collection of pointed tales and reported wonders, the *Travels* owes a lot to *The 1001 Nights*, as well as to the *The Mathnawí* of Jalálu'ddín Rúmí. As for posterity, Orhan Pamuk set his world-art-historical murder mystery, *My Name is Red*, in the Istanbul of Çelebi's first volume.

Born in 1611, Evliya Çelebi was the son of the chief goldsmith to all the Ottoman sultans from Süleyman to Ibrahim; his maternal uncle, Melek Ahmed Pasha, served as grand wazir and as governor of Rumelia (now Bulgaria), Baghdad, Damascus, Van (in the Crimea) and Bosnia. Çelebi studied theology and jurisprudence in *madrese* until the age of 12. He then apprenticed to the personal imam of Sultan Murad IV. By his early 20s, Çelebi was a recognized *hafiz*, reciting the entire Koran from memory in public performances at Aya Sofia, just up the hill from the Topkapı Palace. In 1636, Murad himself took note of Evliya's gifts as *muezzin*, singer and ready wit, and named him a royal entertainer and boon companion.

Çelebi avoided a career at court. Instead, he pursued his lifelong dream of travel, often as an attaché in this or that pasha's entourage. His dream is more than figurative. The *Seyahatname* opens with an account of "a dream of comfort" that came to the young hafiz in a "sleep of wish fulfillment" in 1631, on his twentieth birthday. That night, Çelebi kissed the hand of the Prophet himself, who called him to travel the world, and commanded the youth to record what he would see.

Çelebi's practical curiosity is as universal as ibn Khaldun's; his forty-year travels are sprightlier than ibn Batuta's. Beginning at the Bosporus, the *Seyahatname* touches upon every corner of the Ottoman Empire at the height of its power (excepting the Maghrib), and ends in Cairo, on the River Nile.

As observer, Evliya Çelebi makes no pretense of neutrality. An orthodox Sunni Muslim, his contempt for almost everyone—Christians, Jews, Shi'ites, Zoroastrians, Hindus, Kurds, Franks, Arabs—accounts for much of his narrative's charm, and even guarantees its integrity.

Passing through Safed in Canaan, he describes the language of the Jews, "an ancient and accursed people." Çelebi explains that the two books revealed to this religious community are the Book of Psalms, which God revealed to the prophet David, and the Torah, revealed to Moses. Psalms is entirely prayers, while the Torah, the traveller writes, "is entirely promise and threat, command and prohibition, narrative, permitted and forbidden, paradise and hell and purgatory, resurrection and judgement.... Aside from the Jews, among the Christians as well—the infidels of Sweden, Holland, Dunkerque, Denmark, Germany, etc.—they all read the Torah and the Psalms and they speak Jewish." (By Jewish, Çelebi meant Yiddish, or rather, Ladino.)

His description of the Armenians includes a brief cultural survey: Amalek created the Armenian language; the Armenians are all Christians who follow the Gospel, and are divided into seven sects. "Only their false doctrines," says Çelebi, "are not like those of the Greeks. The Armenians eat oily foods on the eve of the Christian Festival of the Egg (Easter), while the Greeks eat oily foods on the following morning, according to their false fast."

Evliya allows that every world traveller should have a smattering of Armenian to satisfy his needs, and to keep on good terms with the natives. His handy vocabulary transliterates numbers from one to twelve, lists the words for bread, water, raisins, apple, come, and go. The traveller's phrasebook deals with such question-and-answer situations as demanding and failing to be served barley—which exchange concludes with "Go get some or I'll fuck your wife." Other interactions tell other stories: "Come let's go to the garden and drink wine;" "My hero, I love you very much;" "Give me a kiss O my dear boy;" "My hero, what ever happens will happen tonight, come let's go to bed."

When Çelebi accompanied Melek Ahmed Pasha to Split, in Croatia, he encountered the Frankish tongue. According to him, all the Franks speak their own dialect of Italian, and require translators to communicate with each other. He concedes that the Venetian language is most eloquent, then invokes the old saying, "Arabic is eloquence, Persian is elegance, Turkish is an offence, and all other languages are filth."

Vienna posed the Muslim traveller real difficulty. A bronze white elephant clock that struck the hours, a gilded copper peacock that flapped and shrieked, and a pair of cast rams used to execute criminals left him torn between graven imagery and admiration. The elephant's behavior was like that of the black elephant, Çelebi explained, "but it is white magic, a masterpiece of art, that astonishes the viewer."

To qualify the wonder, this orthodox Sunni placed his extended description of Vienna's Stephansdom under the heading, "Dispraise of the cathedral of priests and monks," which he further characterized as a "house of mis-worship the un-good work of a non-upright king."

Yet Çelebi couldn't contain himself. "The paintings and gildings are strange and wondrous works of magic in the Frankish style.... This great cathedral glitters like the gold mine of Mt Akra in Kurdistan and dazzles the eyes like a mountain of light." And several pages later, "When one sees the depiction of Paradise in this Stephan Church..., one wishes to die and go to heaven.... When it comes to painting, the Franks prevail over the Indians and Persians." And then there were paintings of Hell and Purgatory. "Seeing these figures," he wrote, "one's body trembles like an autumn leaf."

There is seeing, and there is hearing.

The Stephansdom's "organ of David" requires 20 priests to operate the bellows. "When the infidels wish to play this organ," Çelebi writes, it takes seventy magicians, "each one a master at the level of Pythagoras," to turn and work its parts. Castrati climb ladders to descend upon the bellows. As they rise and fall, the boys sing along with the organ in voices that will never crack, intoning verses from the Psalter. "According to the Germans' false doctrine," the traveller explains, "while David recited psalms..., he also played the organ.... So when the German priests and monks play the organ...—and the castrati mounted on the two bellows in groups of ten recite the Psalter...—one's lungs fill with blood and one's eyes with tears.... Truly, this organ has an awesome, liver-piercing sound, like the voice of the Antichrist, that makes a man's hair stand on end.... It is only white magic," the Muslim musician concludes, "a concatenation of musical instruments that scatters the wits of the listener."

Volume One of the *Seyahatname* begins with a dream. The last, Volume Ten, starts with what Çelebi calls "Adam's prayer for Egypt in 'Hebrew'." He prefaces his transcription with this account of Adam's wanderings: After the expulsion from Eden, Adam made his first home in Sri Lanka; he next dwelt at Mt. Arafat, then in unfarmed Mecca. Finally, Adam and his descendants went down to Egypt, and settled by the Nile. At first Adam and his (by the Coptic chronicles' count) 40,000 sons lived together in Egypt.

"And this," Evliya Çelebi reports, "is the prayer he recited. It is written in the Hebrew language, because when Adam fell from paradise, in his rebellion he forgot the language of paradise, which is Arabic, and instructed by Gabriel he began to speak Hebrew instead:"

Hidam	My God
tit jedilem	My faith
huji çiji riba	Preserve from the devil
felaj riba felaj riba	Save me, save me
sujüm jaken	All your angels
tarj dilem Serij tena	May they serve me
sija riyeji zehriba	Give wheat I'll make bread
jedilem jiraj jiraj	In the end death occurs, death
Hidam kidam	My God
hirj bijüti jar binti	For my sons this my city
jari mjni jari mjni	Make prosper, make prosper

MUSIC ART

FAR FROM ME: Messiahs

Tradition holds that a messiah is born in every generation.

"Yes," the talmudic sages say. "Let the Messiah come, but not in our time."

Until the messianic career of Sabbatai Ṣevi–historian Gershom Scholem's "Mystical Messiah"–the *Zohar* enjoyed a status equal to the Talmud among learned Jews. But the excesses of the Sabbataian movement left the kabbalist tradition tainted as medieval superstition. And after the English and French Revolutions, modern Jewry sought enlightenment before redemption, citizenship before Jerusalem. Philosophy became preferable to prophecy.

Born in Turkey in 1626, Sabbatai Ṣevi spent much of his adult life oscillating between a luminous conviction that he was the long-awaited Messiah son of David, and profound inner darkness. Hoping to be cured of delusive sickness, in 1665 Ṣevi sought out a young healer of souls, the kabbalist-prophet Nathan of Gaza. Alas, instead of release, Nathan proclaimed the manic-depressive rabbi the Redeemer.

That same year, the newly anointed Messiah delivered a public address (reproduced by Ada Rapoport-Albert in *Women and the Messianic Heresy of Sabbatai Zevi*) on what the Messiah means for the other half of humanity: "As for you wretched women, great is your misery, for on Eve's account you suffer agonies in childbirth. What is more, you are in bondage to your husbands and can do nothing great or small without their consent.... Give thanks to God, then, that I have come to the world to redeem you from all your sufferings, to liberate you and make you as happy as your husbands, for I have come to annul the sin of Adam."

Jews flocked to their new hope. Despite his strange deeds and words, despite the opposition of some rabbis who rejected the Messiah, an army of believers followed Sabbatai Ṣevi's call to march with him to Constantinople. There, he said, he would receive the earthly crown of Empire from the Turkish Sultan Mehmed IV, and so bring on the new order. In 1666, a year of astrological portent, the mystical messiah was arrested outside the Ottoman capital. Called to an audience before the Grand Turk, Sabbatai took the turban.

The Jewish Messiah's apostasy to Islam was enough to disillusion many of those who thought the promised time had arrived. Not to mention those who always doubted. In November 1666, Rabbi Joseph Halevi sent a letter to Jacob Sasportas of Hamburg. He observed that a full year had passed since dispatches from Alexandria, from Egypt, from the Holy Land, from Syria and from all Asia, announced that redemption was at hand. "This good news was brought us by a brainless adolescent from Gaza, Nathan the Lying Prophet," Halevi wrote, "who, not satisfied with proclaiming himself a prophet, went on to anoint king of Israel a coarse, malignant lunatic whose Jewish name used to be Sabbatai Ṣevi."

For those able to weather their disappointment, Nathan of Gaza justified this abandonment of faith on kabbalistic grounds. The Torah is now void. Words have no meaning, except what we say they mean. Bad is now good, good evil. The Messiah must sink low in order to mount high. And so forth. Some of the faithful remained faithful.

Six years after Sabbatai Ṣevi's death in 1676 in Alkum [Dulcigno, Montenegro], Sabbataian devotee Joseph Karillo and a companion called on Abraham Miguel Cardozo in Constantinople. Cardozo was a Catholic convert to Judaism who accepted the Turkish-born messiah, and claimed a messianic role of his own.

The companion recounted for Cardozo their final audience with Sabbatai Ṣevi. "After the New Year [Rosh Hashanah]..., he took us out to the seashore with him and said to us: 'Each of you go back home. How long will you adhere to me? Until you see the rock that is on the seashore, perhaps?' And we had no idea what he was talking about. So we left Alkum, and he died on the Day of Atonement [Yom Kippur], early in the morning...."

A Sabbataian sect practices their version of Judaized Islam in Smyrna to this day.

Moshe Idel, the modern Israeli scholar of kabbalism, interprets history as a kind of sacred text, written in glyphs or emblems as well as in narrative. This method follows a path trod by the Renaissance philosopher of history Giambattista Vico, by the 20th-century essayist Walter Benjamin, and by Benjamin's cousin Gershom Scholem. They assume that events, like words, conceal meaning. Thus, the fact that Sabbatai Ṣevi was born on the Ninth of Av, the day both Temples fell, 1626, is a sign, and not only to the orthodox.

As Abraham Cardozo put it: "What save sadness did Sabbatai, who was born on a funeral day, predict? He was unfortunate in his very name, since, in the Hebrew language, Saturn is called Sabbatai, a sad and malignant star...."

Or as Gershom Scholem wrote in a poem from 1933:
> In days of old all roads somehow led
> To God and to his name.
> We are not devout. We remain in the Profane,
> And where 'God' once stood, [now] Melancholy stands.

Abraham Miguel Cardozo was born in 1630, in Portugal. His family were Marranos, or secret Jews. Raised Catholic and educated at Spanish University, Cardozo left home after graduation to join his brother in Venice. There, he converted (back) to Judaism. A fervent scholar of Judaica, Cardozo identified himself with the Messiah the son of Joseph, a figure who traditionally heralded rather than followed the Messiah from the line of David.

Cardozo accepted the Mystical Messiah, but did not follow Ṣevi into Islam. Indeed, he neither wanted nor expected Sabbatai to bring the Jews back to the Holy Land. "When the Redeemer comes," Cardozo wrote, "the Jews will still be living among the Gentiles even after their salvation is accomplished. But they will not be dead men, as they had been previously." As in the 19th-century dream of Enlightenment, through redemption Jews will experience happiness, and enjoy dignity and honor.

Cardozo's dissent, like Nathan of Gaza's, is rooted in the *Zohar*. But the Sephardic exile's vision faces forward to William Blake's irascible God and the Marriage of Heaven and Hell, rather than backward toward Andalusia, Moses de Leon, and the Zoharic circle of Simeon ben Yohai.

David J. Halperin summarizes the Marrano's minority theology in his edition of *Abraham Miguel Cardozo: Selected Writings*:

> The world hosts four basic religious systems: Absolute, Prophetic Monotheism (Judaism and Islam); Philosophical Deism; Christian Trinitarianism; and pagan polytheism. *All four are false religions.* Muslims and Jews insist that there is no God except the being philosophers call the First Cause. Yet the message that Moses brought to Israel, when he came to redeem them from Pharaoh, was that there *is* a God other than the First Cause. He is the God whom the Bible calls by the sacred four-letter Name, whom the ancient rabbis called the Blessed Holy One.

Where Sabbatai Ṣevi sounds grandiose, Cardozo's voice is modest and extreme. "I am no Messiah," he wrote later in life. "But I am the man of whom the Faithful Shepherd [Moses] spoke when he addressed Rabbi Simeon ben Yohai and his companions: 'Worthy is he who struggles, in the final generation, to know the Shekhinah [the female side of the Divine Presence], to honor Her through the Torah's commandments, and to endure much distress for Her sake.'"

Abraham Cardozo outlived his fallen messiah by thirty years. Addressing Ṣevi's failure to reappear, Cardozo explained that "Our ancient rabbis have said that King Messiah will tell every Jew who his father is, that is to say, his Father in heaven, God, whom they have forgotten in their exile. Sabbatai Ṣevi has not done this. He has not openly proclaimed to the Jewish people the divinity of the Shekhinah, the existence of the Great Name, the truth of God. Even if he was aware of all this, his awareness was for himself alone...."

Jacob Frank was another messiah successful for himself alone. Born in 1726, this Polish Jew with a knack for commerce found his calling in mid-18th-century Smyrna. By force of personality, Frank assumed his messianic mantle in the Ottoman Sabbataian community. This messiah's revealed truth identified four aspects of holiness: the God of Life, of Wealth, of Death, and the God of Gods. Frank lived like an Oriental potentate on the offerings of his followers as he progressed from Turkey through Anatolia to Poland and Bohemia, all the while promising everlasting life on this earth to those numbers of Sephardic and Ashkenazic Jews he converted—to Catholicism.

Frank's converts assumed Polish names and received aristocratic patents when they followed their redeemer into the Catholic Church. Frank identified his daughter—born Rachel Frank in 1754 and later known as Eva—with the Shekhinah, as well as with the Madonna. The Frankists addressed Eva as 'The Maiden' or 'The Virgin.'

Frank's sayings and stories are compiled in a book, *The Words of the Lord*. There, the master asks, "How could you think that the messiah would be a man? That may by no means be, for the foundation is the Maiden. She will be the true messiah. She will lead all the worlds."

Paweł Maciejko calls his Frankist history *The Mixed Multitude*, alluding to both the generation that followed Moses out of Egypt, and to the rising tide of spiritual and political democracy. Witnesses withheld their hosannahs.

A contemporary rabbi's account of one early Frankist-cum-Sabbataian ritual in Lanckoronie, Poland, in 1756, reads like a scene from Isaac B. Singer's *Satan in Goray*: "And they took the wife of a local rabbi (who also belonged to the sect), a woman beautiful but lacking discretion, they undressed her naked and placed the Crown of the Torah on her head, sat her under the canopy like a bride, and danced a dance around her. They celebrated with bread and wine of the condemned, and they pleased their hearts with music like King David...and in dance they fell upon her kissing her, and called her 'mezuzah,' as if they were kissing a mezuzah."

The outside world also took note of Jacob Frank. A 1759 issue of the English *Gentleman's Magazine* featured an anonymous "Friendly Address to the Jews." Its author expressed surprise at a report "that some thousands of Jews in Poland and Hungary had lately sent to the Polish bishop...to inform him of their desire to embrace the Roman Catholic Religion." The correspondent suggested that if you think that the Christian religion is true, and believe the messiah is already come, then when why not "embrace the Protestant religion, that true Christianity which is delivered to us... without the false traditions and wicked intentions and additions of the Popes, who have entirely perverted the truth, and corrupted primitive Christianity."

Overtly Catholic, the Frankists also kept Jewish feasts and holy days. A few years after The Maiden's death in 1816, a secret society, called the Asiatic Brethren of Bohemia, Poland and Hungary, mirrored the Frankists. These Masonic Protestants celebrated Christian holidays as well as the birth and death of Moses, and Shavuot, "to bring about religious unity by leading Christianity back to its Jewish form."

In his table talk, Frank dismisses Jewish worship and tradition with a wave of his hand: "All the Jews are seeking something of which they have not the slightest inkling. They have a custom of reciting every sabbath: 'Come, my beloved, to meet the bride', calling out 'Welcome' to the Maiden. This is all mere talk and song. But we pursue her and try to see her in reality."

"The whole *Zohar* is not satisfying for me," he announced, "and we have no need for the books of Kabbalah." Perhaps Frank forswore more than Jewish mysticism, since "kabbalah" can simply mean tradition.

As for his scriptural forebears, Frank models his conduct after an alternative Lawgiver: "Moses did not die but went to another religion and God permitted it. The Israelites in the desert did not want to walk that road, and when they came to...bitterness, they became aware of that freedom and it was in that place where there was no obligation...."

What of Frank's own place in suspended history? "All religion, all laws, and all the books published up to now as well as whoever reads them, are like reflections of words that died a long time ago. All that comes out of Death. The wise man's eyes should always look to the person in front of him. This man does not look left or right or to the back, yet everybody turns his eyes towards him."

Just before his own death in 1791, Frank announced: "I tell you, Christ is known to you as coming to liberate the world from Satan's hands, but I came to liberate you from all laws and statutes that existed up to now. I have to destroy them all, and only then will God reveal himself...."

MUSIC ART

In *The Poetry of Kabbalah: Mystical Verse from the Jewish Tradition*, Peter Cole translates a popular hymn by Yisrael Najara that is still part of mainstream Jewish worship. The song, "Your Kingdom's Glory," was adopted by Sabbataians as an anthem of messianic kingship. Its seven stanzas were chanted in the Cathedral of Lublin in the presence of Jacob Frank. The hymn begins:

> Let your Kingdom's glory be revealed
> over a poor and wandering people,
> and reign, Lord who has ruled forever,
> before the reign of any King.

Stanza four, the song's center, states:

> I hope for the time of your redemption
> and wait with patience for your salvation.
> If it tarries, Lord, in your absence,
> I will look for no other King.

The plea concludes:

> Bring my people back to you There [Sion's mountain],
> and I will rejoice around your altar.
> With a new song, I will offer
> thanks to you, my Lord and King.

More precise and moving, Cole's verse-paraphrase of one passage from the *Likutei Amarim Tanya* of Rabbi Schneur Zalman, an hasidic contemporary of Jacob Frank, embodies the messianic fervor merely alluded to in the earlier, generic hymn:

> All before Him is as nothing:
> The soul stirs and burns
> for the precious glory of His greatness,
> to behold the light of the King
> like coals of the fierce flame rising.
> To be freed from the wick
> or the wood to which it clings.

Historically, Christians are vexed with the Jews, who insist on waiting for their own messiah, amid discussion of how he will be known, what marks he shall bear both in the scriptural and in the worldly sense, and when. Islam, too, looks for the Mahdī and a day of salvation. Yet even those who believe that their messiah has appeared await a second coming.

So the question of who and what to accept, of how to recognize the truth, abides. I must ask it of myself, if I ask it of others: How could you believe? or, How could you not?

Considering the matter of the pretender, or the fallen Messiah, the question changes: How could a person be so false, and yet walk the earth?

Legend tells that on the day the Temple was destroyed, the redeemer was born. At that very moment, a certain Jew was plowing his field, and his heifer lowed. A passing Arab said, "Weep, Jew. Your Temple is destroyed. I know this from your heifer's moo."

The heifer lowed again. The Arab said, "Rejoice, for the Messiah, who will deliver Israel, is born."

The Jew asked the Messiah's name and birthplace.

The Arab answered, "Menachem (the Comforter) son of Hezekiah, in Bethlehem."

The Jew sold everything, became a garment merchant, and travelled until he reached Bethlehem. Women flocked to buy his wares, and urged Menachem's mother to buy a little something from the merchant. She replied, "Better to have Israel's enemies strangled, than to buy one rag for such a son. The day he was born was the day the Temple was destroyed."

The Jew who came so far to find her said, "It may have fallen on the day your son was born, but I am certain that on his account the Temple will be rebuilt. Take what you need. I will come again, and you will repay me."

Time passed. The Jew returned to Bethlehem, and sought out Menachem's mother. "So tell me, how is your son?"

The woman answered, "Right after you spoke to me, a windstorm snatched him from my hands and carried him off."

So it is said in the Book of Lamentations: Menachem the Comforter is far from me.

CREDITS

"Touching the Present" published by *Forward.com*, September 8, 2017, as "A Month After Charlottesville, A Synagogue Lay Leader Reflects On The Shabbat Of Terror."

"Knowledge and Music" published in *First Things*, June/July 1996, number 64, as "Homer for Today."

"Down to the Sea in Ships" published in *The Weekly Standard*, August 31, 1998, volume 3, number 48.

"Monotheism in Word and Music" published in *The Weekly Standard*, February 22, 1999, volume 4, number 22, as "Moses at the Met."

"The Great Good Place" published in *The Weekly Standard*, May 3, 1999, volume 4, number 31, as "Twelve-Tone Tragedy."

"Unquiet Souls," published in *The Weekly Standard*, August 2, 1999, volume 4, number 43, as "Under Western Eyes."

"Springtime for Wagner" published in *The Weekly Standard*, March 27, 2000, volume 5, number 27.

"Chewing Gum" published in *The Weekly Standard*, September 25, 2000, volume 6, number 2, as "The Good, the Bad, and the Extraneous."

"Eye Altering" published in *The Weekly Standard*, April 16/ April 23 2001, volume 6, number 30, as "William Blake, Burning Bright."

"Into Egypt" published in *The Weekly Standard*, October 1, 2001, volume 7, number 3 as "Picturing Egypt."

"Perfection. Desire. Regret." published in *The Weekly Standard*, September 30, 2002, volume 8, number 3, as "Courtly Love."

"Gum Arabic" published in *Books & Culture*, September/ October 2003, volume 9, number 5, as "After Babel."

"Turkish Modern" published in *Books & Culture*, November/December 2004, volume 10, number 6, as "Pre-emptive Prophecy."

"The Original True History" published in *Books & Culture*, September/October 2005, volume 11, number 5, as "The Exasperated Knight of the Sorrowful Face."

"The Service" published in *Books & Culture*, November/December 2005, volume 11, number 6, as "Fire Consuming Fire."

"Concealed, Revealed" published in *First Things*, November 2006, number 167, as *The Zohar*.

"Chineseness" published in *Books & Culture*, September/October 2007, volume 13, number 5, as "Tangy."

"Plainclothes Policemen of Language," published online in *Books & Culture*, November 24, 2008, Book of the Week, as "Who Is This Writer? How Does He Know Me? An encounter with Roberto Bolaño."

"When Milton Says 'Sing'" published in *The Weekly Standard*, December 1, 2008, volume 14, number 11, as "Happy Birthday, Milton."

"Avatars of True Feeling" published in *Books & Culture,* May/June 2010, volume 16, number 3, as "How Poetry Began with Grief."

"An Old Man" published in *Books & Culture,* March/April 2011, volume 17, number 2, as "On the Way."

"Turkish Classic" published in *Books & Culture,* November/December 2011, volume 17, number 6, as "A 17th-Century Turkish Traveler."

"Far From Me" published in *Books & Culture,* May/June 2013, volume 19, number 3, as "Far from Me: On messianic unease."

ALSO BY LAURANCE WIEDER

Isaiah's Closing Arguments: A New Translation, Highland Books, 2019

After Adam: The Books of Moses, Highland Books, 2019

PoemSite: Songs in the Landscape, Omerta Publications, 2015

Perek Shirah: A Chapter of Song, Omerta Publications, 2013

Words to God's Music: A New Book of Psalms, Eerdmans, 2003

The Poets' Book of Psalms, Oxford, 1999; HarperCollins, 1995

The Red Sea Haggadah, Wiseacre Books, 1995

Chapters into Verse: Poetry in English Inspired by the Bible, 2 volumes (with Robert Atwan), Oxford, 1993; 1 volume selected version, 2000

The Last Century: Selected Poems, Pan Picador MacMillan Australia, 1992

Duke: The Poems as told to Laurance Wieder, Wiseacre Books, 1990

No Harm Done, Ardis, 1975

The Coronet of Tours, Ithaca House, 1972

www.ingramcontent.com/pod-product-compliance
Lightning Source LLC
Chambersburg PA
CBHW020411080526
44584CB00014B/1270